FRIENDS for LIFE

FRIENDS *for* LIFE

JIM & SHEILA COLEMAN

FOREWORD BY ROBERT SCHULLER

WORD PUBLISHING
Dallas·London·Vancouver·Melbourne

Library of Congress Cataloging-in-Publication Data:

Coleman, Jim, 1949–
    Friends for life : building a loving and lasting relationship
    with your mate/ Jim and Sheila Coleman.
    p. cm.
    ISBN 0-8499-3351-X
       1. Marriage—Religious aspects—Christianity.
2. Coleman, Jim, 1949– 3. Coleman, Sheila Schuller.
I. Coleman, Sheila Schuller. II. Title.
BV835.C593 1992
248.8'44—dc20 91–39911
                                           CIP

2 3 4 5 9 LB 9 8 7 6 5 4 3 2 1

Printed in the United States of America

To
Jason James Coleman
Christopher John Coleman
Scott Anthony Coleman
Nicholas Sean Coleman

We dedicate this book to you, our four
precious sons, with the hopes and prayers that
our friendship with each other and with you
and with our Heavenly Father will help you in
your search for your friends for life.

Contents

Acknowledgments   vii
Foreword   ix
Introduction   xiii

Part 1
Through It All
Being Friends for Life Means Living Out Our Commitment—No Matter What

1	Friends for Life!	5
2	Look How Far We've Come	10
3	An Answer to Prayer	14
4	Glow-in-the-Dark Times	19
5	First Things First	25
6	Growing Through a Crisis	28
7	No-Lunch Policy	35
8	Through Thick and Thin	38

Part 2
Listening with Our Hearts
Being Friends for Life Means Moving Toward Understanding

9	Alternatives to Being a Nag	47
10	Men and Women—Appreciating the Differences	52
11	More TNT	57
12	Too Late? Too Old? To Be a Hero	62
13	My White Knight	66

14	Contradictory? Or Complementary!	**71**
15	Some Things Are Better Left Unsaid	**76**
16	Important Clues	**80**
17	Self-Esteem	**85**
18	Listening with Our Ears, Our Eyes, Our Heart	**90**

Part 3

All Things Being Equal
Being Friends for Life Means Giving and Accepting Support

19	Love Lifted Me	**101**
20	Equality? Or Equilibrium?	**107**
21	I Need Help!	**110**
22	Like a Precious Teacup	**114**
23	Can Wedlock Survive Deadlock?	**118**
24	Life's Little Surprises	**123**
25	Married! A New Name! A New Identity!	**127**
26	Who's in Control Here, Anyway?	**131**
27	Response-Ability	**136**
28	And Seldom Is Heard a Discouraging Word	**140**

Part 4

Give It Time
Being Friends for Life Means Giving a Priority to Our Relationship with Each Other and with God

29	Date Night	**149**
30	Repaired for Christmas	**153**
31	Even Grandmas Make Mistakes	**157**
32	Make a Memory	**162**
33	Play, Pray, Pay	**166**
34	All Work and No Praise!	**171**
35	Lost and Found	**175**
36	To the Prettiest Girl in the Restaurant	**179**

Acknowledgments

This book never would have been possible without the positive role models that our parents, Robert and Arvella Schuller and James and Jeanne Coleman, have provided. You four people, more than anyone else, showed us day after day how good marriages are made.

In addition, we need to thank Ernie and Pauline Owen who approached us time after time and asked us to write this book (against our better judgment). When we got discouraged and were tempted to quit, you two friends kept encouraging us and gave us the time we needed to do it right.

Finally, we owe so much to Pastor Dick Klaver, his wife, Kriste, and the Family Life Class at the Crystal Cathedral. A family therapist, a pastor, and our good friend, Dick has taught us so many simple skills that have made our marriage richer and stronger. Thank you, Dick, for four years of "Ahas!"

Foreword

I shall never forget the sunny morning when my oldest daughter—well into her twenties—suddenly allowed her deep disappointment to erupt. She and I were alone at the breakfast table. She looked across her cereal into my eyes, weeping as she asked me, "All I want is a man who will treat me like a precious gem. I think I deserve that, don't I, Dad?"

I cried with her. My heart broke with hers. "Yes, Sheila, you do deserve that." I dried my tears and reached across the table. There was little more I could do, except that we held hands and prayed. "Dear Lord, find the right man for Sheila; she deserves a good one."

Meanwhile, I received news of a new man who had been hired at our ministry to do all the artwork. I didn't think much of it until we got an anonymous telephone call. "Dr. Schuller, you should know that the young artist you just hired is not a practicing Christian. I don't think you want to keep him in your employment."

Well, his position was an important one, and this phone call made me a little uneasy. I felt I should meet him. I shall never forget the day he walked into my office. His long hair, his long mustache, his avant garde glasses, his choice of clothing. All of this reflected the nonreligious young people of the day. And it made one statement: "I am not a practicing Christian."

At that very moment, I had an enormous spiritual compulsion which I immediately interpreted as a message from God: "Schuller, your ministry is trying to reach the nonpracticing Christians and turn them into positive believers. If you are faithful to this ministry, you should have this man on your staff and put him in a position where he can see how the ministry really works. After a matter of months or a few years, if he doesn't become a Christian, you'd better examine your ministry and your own heart and soul deeply and sincerely."

As a result, I viewed this young man as a challenge to my own faith and to my religious lifestyle. Fortunately, he was assigned to share a small office with my wife. Meeting her day after day, week after week, exposed him to a woman in whose heart and life Jesus really lived. He was subsequently invited to a Bible study group led by one of our ministers. Then, to my astonishment, I heard he was joining the church. After working at the ministry for two years, Jim Coleman had discovered the reality of the living Christ.

No one told him to make any changes in his outward lifestyle. Jesus Christ became his personal Lord and Savior. He cut his hair. He bought a suit, complete with shirt, tie, and vest. And he joined the church one beautiful Sunday morning to confess his Christian faith, which he had found in this ministry.

Now the girls began to notice him, including my daughter, Sheila. They had been good friends; indeed, I had watched them work together for more than three years. Then one day, at a Christmas party, the sparks of love were kindled. Jim noticed Sheila as if for the first time. He saw deep spiritual qualities that were the taproots of her character. That was the beginning of a courtship that continues today.

The wedding was beautiful. Their marriage is an inspiration, and today they are the parents of four sons. Nothing is more enjoyable than to visit in their home and see them gather around the table preparing for a breakfast or a dinner. They eat together. They talk together. They share their joys and their dreams together. They set their goals with each other. They are honest and open with each other. They have taken the positive Christian faith that they've heard from our church and are living it out with hope and joy.

If I could have drawn a blueprint of the character I could pick as the husband for my daughter, Sheila, and the father of my four grandsons, I couldn't have drawn one as brilliant and beautiful as Jim Coleman.

There isn't a doubt in my mind that they shall be friends forever. Their marriage is a super success. Their family is a true family. I cannot be more proud of anything that I've been attached to than I am of the family of Mr. and Mrs. James Coleman. I am so excited that they want to share their secrets of a true marriage that will go on until the end of their lives.

This is a book where they share their hopes and their hurts, their dreams and their disappointments. My prayer for you is that God will bless you as you read this book. May you be encouraged and inspired by their honesty, their enduring belief in love, and their commitment to their Lord and to each other.

Robert H. Schuller

Introduction

Marriage—it has been much harder than either of us ever dreamed it would be—and much more rewarding. When we tied the knot we knew that we were embarking on a lifetime friendship.

We knew that we would be together forever—no matter what—because *we were committed to each other, we were committed to the marriage, and we were committed to God.* Sure there were times when we were first married when there were silent, unspoken doubts. Did we make a mistake? But God would remind us that we were committed to each other. That question was no longer viable. "Move on," He'd say. "Don't waste time worrying about that issue anymore. Get on with the work and the rewards of the relationship."

We knew that in order to make it work *we would need to give the relationship a top priority.* We had seen marriages torn apart by in-laws, by money, by hectic schedules, by demands and needs of children. We had also seen marriages survive the business of life when couples had refused to surrender leadership of their marriage to the tyranny of the calendar. We decided to model our marriage after those marriages which had made the relationship a top priority. And, in so doing, we committed ourselves to a once-a-week date night.

We did *not* know how difficult the communication aspect of the relationship would be. It was easy to talk when we were dating and engaged. That's because we never had to talk about difficult things. That all changed, much to our surprise, once we had to live together. Suddenly, we encountered topics that were painful, emotionally charged, and threatening. We tried several methods of communicating, including avoidance, in the process of learning how to talk to each other about touchy subjects.

We also had no idea how difficult it would be to find the delicate balance of equality in our relationship. Idealistic expectations blurred the issues until we sorted through the images that the media had bombarded us with. Only then were we able to see who we really were, who we really wanted to be, and who we could be with God's help.

Through it all, we have had to listen to each other, give each other time, support each other, relinquish our need to control, and forgive each other. There have been fun times, happy times, painful times, silent times, lonely times. Through the years we have grown apart and together. Sometimes we each need our own space; other times we may need the other to reach out to us. Sometimes we need to give support and other times we need to accept support.

Our marriage has been a delicate balancing act, requiring each of us to use a sixth sense to detect what the other partner needs. Sometimes the sailing is smooth. We cherish those times and rejoice in them. Sometimes we've managed to make it across the difficult passages, and other times we have fallen flat on our faces. But we always get up and give it another shot. We absolutely refuse to give up on our love. Our marriage is a lifetime commitment.

We have seen so many—too many—marriages die. Winter blew through a home, and the couple was unable or unwilling to rekindle the spark of love. They couldn't revive the warmth of the relationship. Focusing on the negatives, on what their relationship lacked, they allowed their friendship to succumb to the blight of divorce. We believe this is the greatest tragedy any family can ever encounter.

Whenever we see or hear of Christians going through a divorce, we find ourselves thinking of a story Sheila's father told the family when they were growing up. When Dr. Schuller was a boy, he was helping his father one winter on the Iowa farm. They were busy cutting down a tree that was brown and void of life. The icicles that hung like crystal decorations from the barren branches, shook loose with every blow from the ax and fell to the ground where they splintered.

The frozen tree shuddered and finally fell with a thunderous crash. Both Grandpa and Dad stood clear of the mighty beast as it fell to earth. After the snowy dust had settled, the two farmers went over to examine their work. Grandpa looked at the massive stump, all that remained of the once lush tree. Suddenly, noticing a green ring at the center of the stump, he exclaimed, "Oh Bob! Look! This tree wasn't dead! It wasn't dead! It was just dormant! There is still life in this tree!"

They looked at the tree that lay in ruins. The years that it had taken for it to grow were snuffed out. Now the tree was only good for a chopping block and firewood. No longer would it provide shade for the family or shelter for birds and their nests.

Grandpa looked sadly at Dad and said, "Bob, let this be a lesson to you. Never cut a dead tree down in the wintertime!"

Just because a marriage relationship is struggling doesn't mean that it is dead. Don't give up until every resource has been tapped. Don't give up in the wintertime. Spring may be just around the corner, and if you can keep hanging in there, you may be surprised to find that there is life after all.

There have been mornings when we barely say good-bye as we go our separate ways. The air is still crackling with unresolved anger. Those are tough. Who will make the first move? Why bother? We've traversed this path before. Can't we grow beyond this? But then in the middle of an anguished day the phone rings. Yes. One of us has reached out to the other. "I'm sorry. I love you." Oh, it feels so good to feel the love surge through our hearts once more.

God has commanded us to make our marriages work. He has not commanded us to be successful in our careers. He has not commanded that we be successful in our "ministries." But He has commanded that we be successful at marriage and especially at loving: "A new commandment I give to you, that you love one another, as I have loved you." Paul supported this when he wrote, "And now abide faith, hope, love, these three; but the greatest of these is love."

We can find love in other friendships. We both have had friends that we love to meet for lunch or breakfast. We belong to a small care group at our church, and those friendships are precious. We care for these friends, but there is no guarantee that those friendships will be nurtured and kept alive. Friends move away. Interests change. But marriage is a lifetime deal.

Can God command us to love? Can He command us to make relationships work? We think the answer is yes! He can command us to give our marriage everything we've got to make it work. Love is a choice. Keeping a marriage alive is a decision we make. We decide to make it a priority. We decide to give it the time and attention it needs. We choose to reach out in love to our partner. We commit ourselves to focusing on the good we have.

Becoming friends for life in marriage is a process. We each keep doing it, working at it. We didn't wake up the first day of our married life saying, "Now we're friends for life, and we can get on with our lives." Living out our commitment, today and everyday, includes reaching out, giving and getting support, spending time together, making compromises, and forgiving mistakes, applying God's grace to our marriage.

We hope that you will be encouraged to find the good in your own marriage through the stories you will read in this book. This book is not a how-to book. It is just a collection of snapshots, short glimpses of our marriage. The pictures are real. The stories are honest. Don't be surprised if you see your own marriage in these pages. You just might discover that your marriage is normal after all. In the process, we hope that you will be encouraged and inspired to keep working on your own marriage. We both took turns writing these stories. We've given you clues as to whose turn is whose. We also have mixed the stories up. They do not follow a chronological order. Instead we have grouped them into four sections, making four statements about marriage and about being friends for life. We live out our commitment, no matter what. We move toward understanding. We give *and* accept support. We give our relationship—with each other and with God—a top priority.

We are not marriage counselors. We are not family therapists. We are not psychologists. We are just two people who believe that marriage is important. We believe that it can survive the pressures of everyday life. We believe that we can be friends for life—we can be together— forever! We believe in it because it is God's plan for our lives. We glorify Him when we live out His salvation in our marriage. If we can do it, so can you. May this book be an encouragement to you to keep working on your marriage, to keep living out your commitment to each other and to God, to keep on discovering the joy and the rewards of being together forever—friends for life!

Part 1

Through It All

Being Friends for Life Means Living Out Our Commitment — No Matter What

Dear Lord,

As we travel this path of life with its winding, uncertain ways, bind us together forever, friends for life. Spare us from the tyranny of pettiness. Protect us from the wearisome ways of negativity. Open our eyes and our hearts to all the good in each other and all the good that we can be.

We vow to keep our eyes on You—no matter what we may encounter—as we grow through the process of staying together day by day. We do not know what tomorrow holds, but we find comfort in knowing that we need not travel alone.

So, thank You, Lord, for . . .

. . . the gift of our friendship,
. . . the comfort of our companionship,
. . . the security of our commitment
. . . to each other and to You.

May we never forget the vows that made us one, stronger and better than either of us could be alone. Remind us daily to love, honor, and cherish all that we are . . . for richer, for poorer . . . in sickness and in health . . . and 'til death do us part . . . friends for life.

Amen.

Being confident of this very thing, that He who has begun a good work in you will complete it.

Philippians 1:6

1

Friends for Life!

"Thou shalt not commit adultery!"

"What?" I looked at my friend.

Her eyes were twinkling. She said, "Okay, Sheila, how will you handle *Thou shalt not commit adultery?*"

I gulped and muttered, "Good question." I had been toying with the idea of writing a series of children's books based on the Ten Commandments. One of the first steps in the writing process is talking, so I decided to bounce this latest idea off my friend. She repeated her question, "How will you teach the seventh commandment to children? How will you handle the concept of adultery?"

To tell the truth I hadn't really thought about *that* commandment. I had been creating concepts for teaching the other commandments, but I had overlooked this one. "Hmmm . . .," I stalled. "I guess . . . I could . . .," suddenly a phrase popped into my head. I said, "Well, I guess I could talk about moms and dads being friends for life."

My friend slowly turned her face from me. The light-hearted banter ceased. A heavy stillness hung over the tiny room. Something was terribly wrong. I took her hand and said, "What is it?"

She looked up at me with tears swimming in her eyes. She waved her hands at me, as if to say, "Give me a minute. This is too painful."

I waited, alarmed and a little frightened. What was happening? Something I had said had obviously touched a very sensitive spot in her life. What was it?

She wiped her eyes and took a deep breath. She said simply, "My husband and I are having trouble right now—being friends."

As she voiced the feelings I had feared were in her heart, I struggled to find appropriate words. I wanted to take her hand and make everything better. I longed to find the right words, the right bandage with which I could treat her wounds. But that, of course, was only wishful thinking. There are no magic words when a marriage is in trouble. Friends, counselors, and pastors are unable to make a marriage work. The two individuals are the only ones who can make or break a marriage.

As I looked at my girlfriend and groped for words, I thought of my own marriage. Jim is my best and dearest friend. There is no one I prefer to be with over and above my husband. There is no one I trust more than Jim. He is my one essential friend. We have a good, strong relationship. Nevertheless, even our marriage has had its moments!

It's not easy keeping a marriage alive. There have been times when I wondered if my marriage was any good. I've had moments when I was sure our relationship didn't begin to live up to what I had read and heard it was supposed to be. The pressures and demands of living together and working together, keeping our busy lives functioning, often pushed the feelings of love far, far away.

And romance?! Who has time for romance? Babies cry at night. Dishes pile up. The laundry basket is *never* empty! Lunches need to be made in little brown bags. Floors are dirty. (You always know it can't be put off any longer when you're actually sticking to it.) Life is tough.

Preparing dinners has always been the worst. That's when complete pandemonium breaks loose, and babies are the fussiest. When my boys were smaller, I frequently felt like my juggling act was falling apart with balls dropping all around me. It's no easy task, cradling an infant in one arm, with two toddlers wrestling around my feet. Somehow I managed to keep my balance and chop, chop vegetables with my free hand. I would pop the pacifier back into the mouth, but baby pushed it back out. It tumbled to the floor. Just then I heard an ominous hiss from the stove. I lunged to rescue the boiling pot. The phone rang as I heard the car pull into the garage. It's my loving husband! Am I interested in romance? Hardly! I'm interested in a helping hand! Now that the boys are a bit older, the details of the pandemonium are a bit different, but it's still pandemonium.

When Jim comes through the door, weary from fighting traffic and working all day, home to his safe, calm refuge, is he greeted with warm slippers? A pipe? A puppy dog with paper and wagging tail? Quite the contrary! Like a cat stalking its prey I pounce as he opens the door. "Here, Jim! Catch!" I call as I toss him one baby after another.

Life is full, hectic, chaotic when you're married. Real life interferes with romance. Life wreaks havoc with love. It threatens to strangle it. I have four boys. They came in quick succession. I have worked part-time. And I have written books and gone back to graduate school. Jim manages a Little League team. We are living real life, and sometimes it's hard to keep our love alive in it. It's hard to make time for each other. It's easy to let the friendship slide.

There have been overwhelming days when I wanted to chuck it all, pack a bag, get in the car, and drive forever and ever to nowhere. There have been bleak times, when I felt like I was living with a stranger. We were two people dwelling under the same roof, sharing the same concerns, playing on the same team, but ignoring each other's signals.

But those moments pass. It isn't long before I begin to miss Jim's friendship. I long for his companionship. I yearn to hear his laugh, to feel his touch. Then it's as if the blinders come off and one of us will say, "Hey! It's good to see you again. Remember me?!"

I love my husband. I cherish his friendship. Our relationship is my most treasured possession. I would do anything to save it. I would talk to a pastor or a counselor. I would read books. I would get down on my knees and ask God to show me how to renew our love. Why? Because I feel lost, empty, lonely without him.

I looked over at my girlfriend. Words were stuck in my throat. How could I tell her what was in my heart? There was too much to say. So I merely took her hand and said simply, "Don't give up on your friendship with your husband. You can work it out. I know you can. I will pray for you. Don't give up."

As we hugged and parted ways, I felt frustrated, sad, disheartened. Had another marriage bit the dust? Was another couple's love lost forever? Would they work it out? *Could* they work it out? No one knew but them.

I couldn't get her out of my mind. I thought of her often and carried our conversation around in my heart like a burden. I wanted to tell her that I understood. I wanted to tell her that I knew how complicated and frustrating it can be. But I also wanted to tell her, "Never give up, never quit, never turn back." Yes, the journey of marriage is challenging, but it can also be an exciting, fulfilling, thrilling friendship. I'd do *anything* to ensure that Jim and I would be friends for life—that we would be together—forever.

2

Look How Far
We've Come

I looked at the words in hot yellow paint and familiar handwriting, splashed across the rear window of our car: "JUST MARRIED! TWELVE YEARS AGO TODAY!" The whole world can see that I've been married for twelve years and my husband still loves me!

It was the first time we had retraced the steps of our honeymoon. Twelve years ago today we had driven off into the sunset from Los Angeles to San Francisco, following the path of California's Pacific Coast Highway in early spring. There is no more majestic or scenic drive in the whole world. The thundering ocean to the west, redwoods to the east. Fiery patches of iceplant, like splashes of brilliance, are thrust randomly in fields of soft sand. Golden California poppies, by the millions, illuminate the land.

Whereas I had been involved in the planning of the first honeymoon, this second honeymoon was a complete surprise. Jim had given me a card the night before at a surprise birthday-and-anniversary party that told me of his plans. He had arranged for sitters for all four of the boys.

Now, here we were, skimming along in our car, his hand-painted bulletin broadcasting the fact that we were on our second honeymoon. I felt so free. So happy. So loved. Yet there came nagging doubts. There were those spots along the road where we had argued the first time around. Those arguments had haunted me. How would I feel when we retraced those steps? I blocked the fears and pushed them far away. *That was twelve years ago,* I told myself. *Surely whatever bothered me back then is no longer relevant. Forget it. Move on. Just enjoy the gift of a beautiful three-day weekend.*

My own advice was easy to follow. The day was as glorious as I remembered our wedding day had been. There is nothing more spectacular than a sun setting over the ocean. We laughed and talked like young lovers. Amazing, that there was still so much to talk about after twelve years.

It was a fun day. A romantic evening. A relaxing, refreshing weekend. And the more we traveled, the more we talked about that first honeymoon. "That's where we stopped for dinner."

"There's the turnoff for Hearst Castle."

"That's where we had our first fight as a married couple."

Jim said it. He had remembered. Our first fight. "Do you remember what we fought about?"

"Yes. Do you?"

"Yes."

"What do *you* remember about the fight?"

"Never mind. I think it's better left unsaid."

Silence.

"I don't think I want to bring it up again," Jim said, laughing nervously.

"Well . . .," I began, then stopped and on a sudden impulse I blurted out what I had remembered of our first fight. I recounted the conversation that I had carried for twelve years.

Jim said, "Really? I said that? Boy, that was pretty insensitive of me." He laughed. "I can see why that made you mad. I thought we fought about . . ."

And so it went. All the way up the coast. We recounted our first trip to San Francisco together, remembering the good and the not so good. We remembered the tender times and the not-so-tender times. And what amazed me was how much we had grown. Our love had matured and deepened. It had grown richer, stronger. We were more sensitive, more caring. Where we had been insecure and self-centered on our first honeymoon, we were more giving and self-reliant this time around.

San Francisco shone like the jewel I had remembered. We rode the cable cars in the dark of the night, up and down the glittering streets. We hung from the sides like teenagers, the bells clanging, the wind biting through our jackets, the lights of the city spread out like a crazy quilt at our feet.

And Alcatraz. I'll never forget Alcatraz. Our boys had been asking me about this mysterious place. And so I had asked Jim if we could visit this island of intrigue.

"Alcatraz?" he said, eyes wide. "You want to see Alcatraz? Gosh. I've always wanted to see Alcatraz, but I never suggested it because I didn't think you'd like it." He added with a glint in his eyes, "This is almost as good as our first honeymoon when you did anything I wanted you to do with me."

We walked the island hand in hand and heard the stories of Al Capone. We huddled on the ferry. We toured a World War II submarine. We dined on sourdough and clam chowder. We shopped in Ghirardelli Square. And we took in a special exhibit of the Dutch Masters' paintings at the museum in Golden Gate Park.

It was a beautiful, romantic weekend. And it deepened my love for Jim and my faith in our relationship. It reminded me of the romance that had been in danger of being snuffed out by years of diapers, bottles, bills, dishes, piles of laundry. The embers of an affectionate love life were still glowing, and they burst into flames several times that weekend!

What a great gift Jim gave me, a trip down memory lane, remembering past times and making new memories. But it was much more than just a collection of memories. It was a positive assessment, an evaluation of who we are as a couple and how we've progressed. Driving up and down the coast, talking about our relationship for hours on end, thinking about us, analyzing us, I took stock of all the good that we were as a couple.

That was good for us, because often we focus on all that we are not, all that we are doing wrong, and all that we are neglecting. We tend to magnify our mistakes and overlook our successes. That weekend awakened a new appreciation for my husband and for our love and friendship. It opened my eyes to the positive aspects of our marriage.

We have come a long way—as individuals and as a couple. We have learned a lot about each other and about ourselves. We still have a long road ahead, God willing and thank God. We have many more exciting adventures awaiting us. It's fun to look ahead and imagine what's in store, but sometimes it's good to look back and see just how far we've come.

3

An Answer to Prayer

I opened my Bible as I did every morning and every evening since I committed my life to Jesus. A Christian friend had given me a guide, with specified passages to read each day. At the end of the year, I had read through the entire Bible. The next year I repeated my trek completely through God's Word. I was on my third round. Over two years had passed since the day on a bus coming home from a weekend with my "buddies," when I said to Jesus, "I need help."

I had since made many wonderful new friends. I had just started dating Sheila, the "boss's" daughter. I was mindful of a trace of apprehension, but my heart confirmed that my motive was sincere. We had been friends for the past four years. My feelings for Sheila were growing stronger. I was feeling things for her that I had never felt for anyone before. I had actually found myself considering "popping the question."

Since my life was rooted in prayer these days, I had decided to put my faith into action. I had been praying: "Dear God, is Sheila the girl You want me to marry? Is she the one You have in mind for me—to be my wife, the mother of my children? Is she the one I am to spend my entire life with?"

Now I found myself reading the twenty-fourth chapter of Genesis. The heading in the Bible read, "A Bride for Isaac." I read, wide-eyed, as if for the first time, the account of Abraham, well on in life, dying, and concerned because his son, Isaac, did not have a bride. He called his most dedicated servant to his bedside and asked him to return to the land of his forefathers and find the right girl whom he could bring home to marry Isaac.

The obedient servant did as he swore he would do. He traveled to Abraham's homeland. When he arrived at a well, he prayed, "Oh God, when the woman comes to the well who is to marry your servant, Isaac, let her let down her water jug and offer it to me and may she say, *Sir, let not me only provide water for you but let me water your camels as well.*"

To me this obviously meant that he was looking for a woman who was willing to go the extra mile. He was looking for someone who would not only do the obvious in offering a stranger water, but go one step further—who would be gracious enough to offer to satisfy and attend to the needs of his camels as well.

After his prayer, the Bible describes how many young women came to the well. But only one, Rebekah, offered to water his camels after she tended to his needs. He then returned to Rebekah's tent seeking to speak to her father. Her father agreed to send Rebekah back to Israel to marry the son of Abraham. Wow! Here in the Holy Bible was an example of a God-fearing man asking and trusting God to guide him at a crucial time!

Sheila and I had been spending a lot of time with a fantastic Christian couple, Toby and Barb Waldowski. Their Christ-centered marriage had been an inspiration to me. Based on my growing love for Sheila and what I had read in my Scripture reading, I boldly asked God in prayer, "Lord, if I'm to ask Sheila to marry me, if this proposal is ordained by You, Lord Jesus, bring my friend, Toby, into my office this Friday at 10 A.M." I had often heard about being specific in our prayer life, but this was crazy! Once again, a quiet peace dominated my soul. The fleece was out.

Up to that point, Toby had come into my office maybe two or three times a year. The only time I saw him in my office was when he was recording an album. Then he would stop by to ask me to help him with the artwork on the album cover and/or do some brochures or a letterhead or something.

That Friday morning I was sitting in my office watching the clock. At ten o'clock the doorknob turned behind me. I looked around and there stood Toby—an unsuspecting angel to be sure. I jumped up and said, "Toby, do you know what this means?" I shared the whole story with him. I told him I was going shopping for a ring that night.

Did that shopping trip ever feel strange! Walking into the first jewelry store, I felt like the most transparent person in the whole world. Surely, I was the only man who had ever felt this vulnerable. My mouth went dry as I tried to spit it out to the man behind the counter that I would like to look at an engagement ring. I stuttered.

I bought a ring and tucked it into the pocket closest to my heart. I pulled off the freeway three times to look at it on my way home. I couldn't believe my eyes. I put it in a very safe and cherished spot in my condominium, and I asked Sheila to go to dinner with me that week at her favorite restaurant. It was a country French inn. I re-served a corner table, with candlelight. I had read that if you ever want to do or say something tender to your woman, wait until dessert.

My heart was in my throat. The dessert was in front of her. I excused myself to go to the restroom. In reality, I ran out the front door, opened the car, got the ring, put it in my pocket, and came back to the table. I looked her straight in the eye over the candlelight, over her ice cream with raspberries and said, "Sheila, will you marry me?"

She looked at me and said, "What?"

I couldn't believe she wanted me to repeat it. It was hard enough the first time. I gulped and repeated the question. "Sheila, will you marry me?"

She smiled and said, "Yes!"

I asked, "Why did you make me ask you twice?" She laughed and replied, "I've wanted you to ask me for so long, that I was afraid I had imagined it."

My prayer was answered. Specifically. And absolutely. There was never a question in my mind that God had guided me, simply because I had sincerely sought His guidance. Not only did this illustrate the power of prayer to me in a dramatic way, it has on many occasions reaffirmed that *God ordained our marriage.* Forever, for better or worse, in sickness and in health, whenever the relationship gets rocky, and *all* marriages do, separation is not an option. God ordained the union. Ride out the storm, seek new answers to old questions, and keep praying.

Prayer is the rock upon which our entire marriage has been built. It is the solid foundation of our family and our relationship. We end *every* day of our marriage on our knees, at our bedside. It doesn't matter how tired we are. It doesn't matter if we are at odds with each other. We may not be speaking for the moment to each other, but that doesn't keep us from speaking to our Heavenly Father.

We hold hands and pray for our marriage, our children, our friends, our neighbors, our loved ones. It has been revealing for us as we have discovered important feelings about each other and our marriage during our prayer time. In voicing our concerns aloud with each other, to Christ, our loving mediator, the ultimate marriage counselor, we have been surprised by what we have heard our own voices say.

"Dear Lord, help me to be more patient."

"Dear Lord, open my ears, my eyes, and my heart to Jim's needs."

"Dear Lord, forgive me for my insensitivity."

Time and again we have gotten in touch with our feelings and with each other while on our knees in prayer. Frequently, those have been times of readjusting our attitudes toward each other, or recognizing the good that we have, of appreciating what we have been spared from, and of renewing our commitment to each other and to our Lord.

We were brought together, we were bound together, and we remain together by prayer. Prayer has been the glue that has kept us together, through it all, no matter what.

4

Glow-in-the-Dark Times

Most boys love cars. Mine are no exception, including my husband. Cars are his hobby. Since he was fifteen, he has had a "project" car. In reality, it's always nothing more than a dilapidated piece of rusty metal, an engine that doesn't run, seats covered with musty old towels, tires that could possibly be salvaged to use as backyard swings. He's been known to spend a great deal of his time in the garage, pulling out a transmission, draining oil, bleeding brakes, you name it. But when he gets done restoring these old heaps, they're a wonder to behold.

I have absolutely no interest in cars.

Poor Jim. He has explained to me over and over how an engine works. He has patiently pointed out design details that distinguish one model from another. I have heard dissertations on headlights, bumper developments, and car design evolution. Yet with every one of his little lessons I silently ask myself, which is the bumper and which is the fender?

Jim probably spends as much time with his cars as he does with me. And I dare say that they have been just as frustrating for him as I have been. There have been many times when he has emerged from under the hood of a car ready to give up on it. And it's a good thing they have their drawbacks, or I could get really jealous of these sleek beauties with their impeccable paint jobs.

Some of these vehicles have been more challenging rivals than others. Especially those foreign sports cars. Consequently, I am always relieved when Jim wants to trade in one love for a less demanding temptress. Like the little blue Ford.

She sounded good to me when Jim first described her. "She's so cute. You wouldn't believe her," he said. "She's dark blue. Not too big. She's uncomplicated, so she won't cost much."

"What kind of shape is she in?"

"She's beautiful! She's all done. She runs like a top. She's got a fresh paint job, and she's even got new upholstery."

"She's not a project car?"

"No! I like her just the way she is."

"There's nothing about her you wish to change?" (I had to size up this opponent. How much time and work and money would she steal from me?)

"No. She's perfect."

He quickly added, "Come on. Let's take the boys and go look at her. I know you'll like her."

Jim has built-in radar when it comes to used car lots. If you weren't in used-car-intelligence you'd never guess that there was a car lot tucked way back behind those shops. "There she is!" he exclaimed excitedly. He looked hopefully at me. I could almost see his thoughts, *Would I like her, too? Would I agree that we should purchase her and bring her into our home and our lives?*

I am not often impressed with Jim's choices of cars. His taste and mine don't always coincide. But this time I was as taken with the little blue coupe as he was. I was told that she was a '36 Ford. All I know is that I thought she was cute, too. Best of all—she was all done! Her dark blue paint was set off smartly with crisp red pinstriping. She had been carefully restored by the former owner, complete with lush, plush mohair upholstery.

We would get in her and drive away. The boys were absolutely ecstatic. They hopped into the rumble seat and said, "When do we get to buy her?"

The blue coupe looked like a fun way to combine Jim's love for cars with fun family rides in a rumble seat. We took her home and have never regretted it. The Old Car is still a special member of our family. The boys occasionally help their Dad wash and wax her. When she's all cleaned up, she really draws attention.

There's nothing more inviting on a summer evening than piling into the rumble seat, getting ice cream cones, and driving around until the warm night air caresses the boys to sleep. One beautiful summer night we set out to do just that.

Scotty was playing with his new lightstick, one of those plastic tubes filled with fluorescent fluid. Scotty had been begging and begging for one. Jim had picked one up for him on his way home from work that afternoon, and Scotty hadn't been able to put it down.

It was a gorgeous night. The sky was still aglow from the setting sun. Everything was idyllic. The brief moment of tranquillity was broken when Scotty started to cry. "My lightstick! My lightstick!"

To my horror I saw garish yellow goop oozing through his fingers, slipping onto his lap, and soaking into the mohair upholstery. Jim turned white. That little car did the quickest U-turn you've ever seen. It made a bee-line back home. Jason yelled through the back window, "Where are we going?"

"Home!" I hollered. "Scotty's lightstick broke."

Jim was livid. Even though he hadn't said a word, I knew how furious he was. His silent rage filled the car like an ominous cloud. No one dared say a word for fear that the anger would erupt. The boys piled out of the car. I threw rags to Jim, and he set frantically to work. We both had had a lot of experience with such catastrophes. We were gradually becoming accustomed to the stains that go along with being parents. Still, I cringed as I thought of the beautiful mohair that was undoubtedly ruined—not to mention the evening.

Jim worked and worked while I kept a watchful eye on the boys. All of a sudden Jim said, "Well, doesn't anyone here want to get ice cream?"

"You mean we're still going?"

"Sure. Look! I got it all out."

I couldn't believe my eyes. If you had not seen the accident happen, you would never have known that anything had been spilled on that seat. It looked like it had the day we brought it home.

"All right!" the boys yelled. They piled back into the car. "One more try," Jim said. He managed a weak smile. I could tell that it had been all he could do to keep his mood from being shattered.

The rest of the evening went without a hitch. The ice cream was delicious. The drive home was glorious. The sky looked like a child's vivid water color. The bright magentas splashed with yellow across a dusky blue sky. The moment seemed to last for ever. It was a calm, tranquil, peaceful summer sunset. Jim took some side trips, and we talked as the boys drifted off to sleep. I was surrounded by everything and everyone I had ever wanted.

I looked over at my handsome husband. "Boy, that was a close call," I said.

"That's for sure. I couldn't believe my eyes when I saw all that glowing oil seeping into my mohair." Jim shuddered again at the thought.

"I never thought you'd be able to get it out."

"Neither did I." .

"It looks good as new."

"Thank heaven!"

I love those times when the day is almost over and there's just Jim and me again. We have our boys all around us in the car, but there are no interruptions.

It was totally dark by the time we pulled into the garage. The door clanked shut behind us, and we began the task of carrying four little boys to bed. I had tucked the last two in bed and gone back to the garage. Jim was putting two pairs of shoes away. "Are they all in bed?" he asked.

"Uh huh!"

"Well, then, I guess we're done for the evening."

"Yes!" I started back into the house.

Jim turned out the light and turned to shut the garage door. Suddenly, he called, "Sheila! Come look!"

I poked my head back into the dark garage. There, radiating from the front seat of our fun little Ford was an eerie glow. Our car's upholstery was glowing in the dark! Jim had managed to get out the oil. When the lights were on you couldn't even see a ring. But when the lights were turned out it was a different matter. It all showed up in the dark.

I went back from time to time that night to look at

our glow-in-the-dark coupe. It gradually grew dimmer and dimmer. In a way, I wished it would always glow. But it was just a one-night deal.

As funny as it was, that glowing coupe taught me a lesson about life's trials and our faith in God. It occurred to me as I watched that glowing mohair upholstery that faith shines brightest in the darkest times. Faith may be there, but as long as it is in the light it won't show up. Put it in the darkness and watch faith glow bright!

Jesus said, "I am the light of the world" (John 8:12). Jesus promised that His love would shine in the darkness. It's not until we put ourselves or find ourselves in situations where we are put to the test, that our light will glow to the point where others will notice, that others will see that we were able to hang on by faith. In the process, we glow in the dark.

I shudder to think where Jim and I would be without our faith. It has been the framework upon which our entire relationship has been built. If we had tried to stand alone in our faith—we would have easily been overwhelmed by our tough times. But because we are joined together in a common belief, our faith is strengthened like a tempered chain of mail. Our faith is linked, entwined. That way, when one of us is tempted to grovel in the dark, the other keeps the embers alive, keeps feeding the sparks, until we can see the light glow once again. Together our faith is strong enough to glow in the darkest times. Together we can be lights in a dark world. Together we can keep our love and our faith alive—forever!

5

First Things First

Once on the nationally televised "Hour of Power," Dr. Schuller asked Debbie Boone, "Debbie how do you maintain your Christian ideals in the entertainment business, a business that pulls at you in many directions? Isn't it hard?"

I'll *never* forget her answer. "Not when you have your priorities right. When you're committed to your ideals and you have your priorities, every decision is easy. It's either black or white."

I agree with Debbie. When priorities are straight, decisions are as clear as black and white, night and day. I learned how easy it is to make hard decisions early in our marriage.

One night I was walking along a pathway on a golf course. It was late and it was pitch black. I was surprised at how dark it really was. I love to walk late at night in the cool air with millions of stars above me. It helps release stress, and that was the release I needed then.

I was turbulent inside. The more I walked, the more troubled I became. Why was this walk having the opposite effect on me than what I sought?

I began to cry. Tears rolled down my cheeks. I missed my family, my wife and my baby boy Jason, my first son.

Then it happened. I realized when I started to cry that this was the release I had been building up to. "I just want my family around me, Lord. I don't want to leave them."

Earlier in the day I had been putting some finishing touches on a new venture with a business associate. Our plan was to create a series of seminars requiring me to travel more than I usually like to do. The opportunity sounded exciting, fun, growing. So we decided to proceed with our plans.

As the sun set, I found myself alone in a hotel room, and loneliness set in around me. Whom was I kidding? Thinking that I could leave Sheila and my son "frequently" when one night now seemed like forever? When being a hundred miles away for a two-day meeting seemed like being on the other side of the earth?

So I wept and then, only a moment later, rejoiced. My decision had been made. The next day at lunch once again, I looked my budding new business associate in the face and said, "Doug, I can't do it. I'm fooling you and myself to ever think that I could be a 'traveling man.' I barely survived last night away from Sheila and my baby boy. I'm not cut out for extended trips. Forget it!"

That decision was easy to make because Sheila and I have always shared two primary priorities in our married life. One is our commitment to our date night, our time together. Our other priority is our children. I cannot tell you the number of dinner invitations we have refused, the advisory positions with church organizations we have turned down. I've lost count of the opportunities we received to travel, to speak, to participate in worthy, charitable events that we have declined. We said no to many events and opportunities that we were tempted to say yes to. We chose to refuse these invitations because we believe that at this stage in our lives we have been called by Jesus Christ to give our primary devotion to our family, to our children.

We will only have them with us in our home for eighteen years. That is but 25 percent of our years on this earth. Our children were given to us to lavish the attention that only a mother and father can provide. There is no substitute for the companionship, love, security, and strength that Mom and Dad can give.

That is not to say that we have never had dinner out with another couple, or had to travel out of town, or been involved in any outside committees or endeavors. We have. But we keep it to a minimum. And we carefully plan, question, and review the calendar—*together*—before we say yes.

When I do say yes, I must ask myself, how many nights will that be away from home? How many nights will the children go to bed without one of us reading to them? Without one of us praying with them? Without Mom or Dad listening to their last thoughts of the day?

It's easy to think that something or someone else is more important than my children, to feel that somebody else needs me more than they do. But when I keep my primary priority at the top of my planning the decision is always black or white and usually very easy to make. I have chosen to make time with my wife and my children my number one priority, to be together as much as possible—so we can be together forever!

6

Growing Through a Crisis

There was nothing we could do to quiet our feverish child. He cried relentlessly. His breathing was labored, his little chest pulled tightly around his ribcage with every breath. My stomach began to churn. I was growing more concerned by the minute. My fears were shared by the allergy specialist, Dr. Galant, who had been calling regularly for the last two days for an accounting of respiratory rate, temperature, and pulse to check on Christopher's recent battle with asthma. Up until now his temperature had been normal. But it was beginning to rise alarmingly. His little three-month-old body shuddered as the fever shot higher and higher. Just then the phone rang.

"This is Dr. Galant. How's Christopher?"

"He's running a fever."

"How high?"

"104 degrees."

"Bring him to the emergency room. I'll meet you there. I want you to know that I will be arranging for a spinal tap."

I hung up the phone and buried my face in my boy's fevered body. My sobs brought Jim. "What is it?" he asked.

"Dr. Galant wants us to meet him at emergency. They want to do a spinal tap."

"What's that for?"

"It's a test for spinal meningitis." My premed background had given me enough information to make me nervous, not enough to allay my fears.

Our neighbors kindly watched two-year-old Jason while we drove Christopher to the hospital. He cried incessantly, which was so unlike our cheery little bundle of joy. The nurse took him from my arms and told me it would be better if I waited outside while they did the spinal tap.

I hid myself in the tiny bathroom and tried to block out my baby's screams. Jim was there. But I had also blocked him out. I was not in any mood to be comforted. I wanted to purge the grief. I had no strength left to fight the fears. I wallowed in them and allowed them to take over. I gave way to the sobs and let them roll out of my being. The grief engulfed me and carried me into the bowels of pain, fear, and despair. "My baby! My baby! Oh, God please help my baby!"

A hesitant knock on the door brought me back to sanity. "Sheila?" It was Jim's voice.

"I'll be right out."

"Are you okay?"

"I just need a minute."

I washed my face in the sink, drew a deep breath, and faced my husband. Jim, pale and frightened, put his arms around me.

"I'm scared," I said.

"He'll be all right."

"How can you be so sure?" I snapped.

"God will take care of him."

Jim's faith was infuriating. I didn't share his faith right now. All I felt was raw, painful fear. I wanted to fight for my baby, not rest peacefully on faith. I clung to my helpless frustration. As each of Christopher's screams filled the cold corridors, I could feel a fresh surge of adrenaline. I was ready to go to battle for my infant son.

The doctor came out of the room and handed Christopher to me. He wore only a diaper. The band-aid at the base of his spine bore proof of his torture. The nurse said, "Keep him uncovered. It will help the fever go down."

"What about Tylenol?" I asked.

"We can't give him anything that affects the central nervous system. If he has an infection in the spinal fluid, any medication that tampers with the area can have a reverse effect."

"When will you know the results?"

"In about fifteen minutes."

There was no comfort for my baby. I held him on my shoulder. I cradled him in my arms. I walked him, I rocked him. Nothing helped. I glanced at Jim. He looked at me sadly, but I could tell that he was not as worried as I was. He was unhappy, but he was not filled with terror. *How can he sit there so calmly?!* I thought angrily. *Our baby's life is in danger, and he's not the least bit concerned.* None of this was true, of course, but I had to aim my anger somewhere—Jim happened to be the nearest target.

About ten agonizing minutes passed. Finally the nurse called, "Mr. Coleman? Mrs. Coleman?"

"Yes?"

"There are cells in the spinal fluid."

"There are?"

"Yes."

"He has . . ."

"Yes. We are preparing him a bed. It will take us a while to get a room for him in ICU."

"ICU." My head began to spin. It felt like someone had punched me in the gut. I felt nauseous. It can't be happening, I told myself, but the touch of Christopher's feverish body taunted me with the truth.

The nurse led us down one corridor and then another. We walked through big wide doors with huge block letters over them, INFANT INTENSIVE CARE UNIT.

She took my naked baby from me and put him in a crib with cold cagelike bars. She hooked him up to a series of wires. Monitors beeped at me. Needles prodded. Chris continued to cry and cry and cry. How much more can I bear? I leaned on Jim's shoulder, hid my face, and once again gave way to the grief.

The doctors surrounded the crib and conferred. Christopher was not just battling spinal meningitis. His asthma was a major complication. In addition, both ears were infected. Not an easy battle for such a small little life.

"We have decided to treat this as aggressively as we can," Dr. Myers, our pediatrician, said. She had arrived almost instantly. It was comforting to see this team of experts so concerned, moving so speedily and conferring so quickly. "We will give him antibiotics through his IV," she continued. "We will give him medication to ease the asthma likewise through his IV. There is nothing we can give him for the pain."

"Is that why he's crying?"

"Yes. Spinal meningitis is very painful."

"I can't stand to hear him cry."

"It is very hard," the doctor said. "I suggest you go home. Let us take care of him now. It is important that you are rested when we send him home."

"How long will he be here?"

"That depends."

Oh, how hard it is to turn your back on your baby, to walk away from a critically ill infant, whose naked body is traversed with a series of wires, needles, and tubes, whose cries follow you down the hall, down the elevator, through the city, and into his empty bedroom!

I will never forget the empty, hollow feeling of walking into my home without my baby. The house screamed at me, "He's not here! He's not here! He's not here!"

I glanced at his infant seat, where his bright eyes had always followed me. He always waited until I took a moment to notice him, whereupon a radiant smile would beam at me. Now that seat was empty. There was no round, wide-eyed baby. No smiles. No Christopher.

That night, when we went to bed, Jim wrapped me in his arms. He said sadly, "I went down to Christopher's nursery. It felt so lonely without Christopher. I put his little blue Bible in his crib and asked Jesus to take care of him for us."

I cringed at Jim's words. I had always believed in Jesus. Yet, this was *my* baby! I was afraid to let go of him for fear that Jesus would take him back. Jim couldn't understand my uncontrollable fears; I was mystified myself at my lack of faith. I know he was perplexed when I turned my back to him that night and slept with anger and confusion burning in my heart.

Sleep only lasted a few hours. I awoke at four in the morning, my arms aching to hold my son. How was he? Was he still breathing? Was he still crying? Was he still in pain?

I quietly walked the dark hallway and stood by the moonlit crib. I knew that sleep was out of the question, so I went downstairs and sat in the dark family room. I turned on the picture lamp that lit up a favorite painting we have of our Lord. I looked at this picture and prayed, "Jesus, I have never needed You more than I do right now. I am scared. I am afraid. I need to hear You. I need to feel You."

As soon as I prayed those words a calm crept over me. I closed my eyes. A peace that passes understanding filled my mind. And an image began to take shape. I saw Jesus standing, holding my baby. Christopher was wrapped in a soft, cuddly blanket. I heard these words pass through my mind, "You like to take credit for this beautiful baby, don't you?"

I laughed, "Yes, he's beautiful."

"He is beautiful. But he's not just your baby. He's *my* baby, too."

"I know that, but . . ." I couldn't finish my objection for suddenly I realized that Christopher was more at home in Christ's arms than he was in mine. Jesus was holding him just the way I held him.

Suddenly, I felt freedom from my fears. I said, "Okay, Lord. I give him back to You. I don't know what this means. I don't know if You will let me keep him for a while, but I know that either way You will take good care of him."

Christopher made it through. It was a tough battle. He cried until he was hoarse. He was in intensive care for an entire week, and he required physical therapy for three months afterward. There were tough days, but it was much easier to endure because I wasn't fighting against myself, against Jim, and against my Lord. In answer to a sincere cry for help, Christ calmed my fears. He enabled me to believe in His goodness, and He drew Jim and me together, working as a team to make it through a real crisis.

Being friends for life means living out our commitment—no matter what—even through a crisis. When we let go, when we accept Christ's help, we can be more than conquerors. As the Bible says, "Who shall separate us from the love of Christ? Shall tribulation, or distress, or persecution, or famine, or nakedness, or peril, or sword? Yet in all these things we are more than conquerors through Him who loved us" (Rom. 8:35, 37).

Jim and I have learned the hard way that our faith will never fail us if we will only let go and let God carry us in His arms of love.

7

No-Lunch Policy

I couldn't look her in the eye. I felt uncomfortable. I was at lunch alone with a female. She was a friend, a colleague, a business associate. She worked for me. She performed an important function at the office. She was efficient and businesslike.

I always try to use the luncheon hour to accomplish other things than job-related tasks. But I'm aware of the fact that a lunch out is a nice treat for an employee, a nice way for a boss to say thank you. It's great to create an open atmosphere to discuss pertinent business and bolster an employee's attitude. I think I've learned to use the lunch hour in this fashion. It's worked great with the Bobs, Sams, Georges, and Petes. But some small piece *always* felt out of place with the Marys, Sues, Nancys, and Alices.

Fortunately I work around a lot of people who love me, help me, and protect me. I work in a Christian community. We should all be so blessed. One of my supporters brought to my attention that I, as a married man, "had no business going to lunch alone with a female."

I wanted to react harshly when I first received this criticism. But I resisted my temptation to snap back.

Because of the misgivings I had felt at my recent luncheon, I found myself listening instead of defensively shouting, "You don't understand!"

I carried this friend's concern home with me that night.

"Sheila," I said. "It's been suggested that I shouldn't have lunch alone with any women. What do you think I should do?"

My beautiful and wonderful wife wasted no time on this one!

"Whew! I'm so glad you brought it up. I've never liked the thought of you alone with another woman."

I was surprised, but not entirely, as she went on. "When you go to work in the morning and you tell me you're going to have lunch with Mary, I *know* I can trust you. I don't worry about that. But it just doesn't feel right. I guess it almost seems like a date," she said.

Seems like a date. I thought a lot about those words. To this day I can still hear Sheila say them.

I had been on plenty of dates when I was single. Always alone with a girl. Always looking into her eyes, searching, wondering who was in there . . . and in my later years wondering, *Will she be "the one"?*

Now that I've been happily married for twelve years, I'm glad I didn't ambush the loving friend who first brought the topic of lunches alone with women to my attention. I'm glad that I sought out Sheila's advice and feelings. And I'm also glad I gave her the freedom to express her honest views on the subject.

I'm glad I now have my own no-lunch policy and that I *never* go anywhere or spend any time outside the office alone with a woman, whether she's married or not. I've looked across that table. I've sensed how easy it would be to shift the conversation subtly toward more

personal topics. I see now how married people compli-
cate their relationships and create conflicts in their holy
bond by allowing an innocent, unchecked "date" to creep
into their private love affair.

Living out commitment means making choices.
Choices are easy when you are asked to choose between
good and bad. Choices are not as easy to make when they
are between good and better. Those choices take more
thought, more discernment, more prayer. Questions help
me clarify the choices and the directions I will take in my
relationship with Sheila. Questions like, What's *best* for
this relationship? and Will this action threaten the security and the emotional intimacy of our relationship?

It was an easy decision to make in light of these
questions. What's best for my relationship with Sheila is
to keep our relationship exclusive. There are so many
positive alternatives to taking women to lunch alone. I
now take a small group of colleagues out at a time. Actually, it works much better. It's a more economical use
of my time and enables me to safely build professional
camaraderie without putting my marriage or my reputa-
tion at risk.

I mentioned this problem and resolution to another
man I know. He confided, "Now that you mention it, Jim,
I can tell you that my indiscretion in this very area con-
tributed to my divorce many, many years ago."

Sheila and I struggle in our relationship with bills,
children, work, appointments, schedules, emergencies—
the list goes on and on. And during the struggling times
and the good times, there is only one pair of eyes I need
to look into across any table, the eyes of my beloved
wife—now and forever!

8

Through Thick and Thin

I silently slipped out of bed. The alarm hadn't gone off yet. Jim was still sleeping soundly. If I was very quiet, I could get into the bathroom and step on the scale before he could see me.

I tiptoed around the squeaky spots in the bedroom, put my glasses on, and took a moment to get my nerve up. (You know you're really over the hill when you need glasses to read the scale that you don't want anybody else to see.)

I had successfully taken off twenty-eight extra pounds that I had put on with my last baby. I had regained my slender figure, thanks to disciplined dieting and exercising. I managed to keep the weight off for over a year. Then life interrupted and interfered with my exercise routine. My list of excuses got longer and longer. The weight gradually came back. Pound upon pound, it crept back on. Ugh! All that work for nothing! I had managed to deny the ugly facts, but now my condition stared me full in the face. The scale did not lie. Much as I wanted it to. And the truth it told was more than I had feared.

I had gotten a clue the night before when I surreptitiously tried on a skirt that I hadn't worn in a year. The skirt was part of a lovely suit that Jim bought for me to wear to evening events. We were scheduled to attend a charitable event in one week. In my heart I knew the suit wouldn't fit, that the skirt would be too tight. I also knew that Jim would ask me why I wasn't going to wear that suit, and I didn't want to tell him that I had gotten fat—again!

So I waited until he had gone to bed. I got the skirt up over my feet, then my knees; so far so good, then my h-h-hips (Suck it in!). But I still had to zip up the dumb thing. I held my breath as I yanked the zipper up. That skirt was *tight!* I felt my stomach push against every seam. I couldn't believe that this was the same skirt that had draped gracefully around my hips just a year ago. What had I done to myself?!

I slept fitfully. At 3 A.M. I gave in to the sleeplessness, reread my diet book, and started to clean and chop fresh vegetables. I vowed the next morning that I would step on the scale and face the music. So here I was, tiptoeing around, pretending that Jim didn't know, couldn't see that I had put the weight back on. Of course he knew. Of course he cared. So why was I being so secretive?

The plain and simple answer was that I was ashamed. I was disappointed in myself and felt that I had let my husband down. I was no longer the pretty, youthful, slender woman that he had married. I was getting heavy and thick in the waist. (When I am unhappy with my weight, I become overly sensitive to other physical attributes as well.) The mirror these days reflected the lack of beauty sleep, the hours of work, the nights of walking the floor with an asthmatic baby.

Poor Jim! It wasn't fair for him to have to live with this figure. Sure I had always known I would grow old with him, that I would not retain my youthful appearance forever, but I hadn't expected it to go so soon.

Getting dressed in the morning is the worst part of the day when my weight is up. I have to wade through all these clothes that used to fit. I don't believe in throwing away clothes that I've outgrown. That would be admitting permanent defeat. As long as the clothes are in my closet, there's a chance I will lose the weight and wear them again. They are my goal, my inspiration, my destination. They keep me on track when I am tempted to cheat.

I have never been successful dieting without a goal. I have never been successful writing without a deadline. I need goals. I need direction. I need objectives. My marriage needs them too.

Neither of us is the same person we were on our wedding day—physically, emotionally, or intellectually. Jim and I have both grown—in more ways than one! Each of us has faced different situations in our lives; we have been challenged and put in positions where we have grown in our intellectual skills, our thinking skills, and our relational skills. Unfortunately, we have not always grown at the same time or at the same rate. That's life. That's reality.

Because we live in a world that is inundated with a glut of information, opportunities for growth have never been more prevalent. Without a commitment, without a sense of direction, couples can grow in two different directions. They wake up one day and step on the scale to find that they feel like strangers. Is their relationship dead? Is the friendship lifeless? Has the marriage been snuffed out?

Jim and I have made a commitment to our marriage, to our friendship, to our love. That means that we have drawn up a road map. We have chosen the same destination, a common goal. We know what our goals are for our boys. Our goals for our boys are to be responsible, self-sufficient, contributing men of God. We also want them to experience the love, the grace, and the joy that comes from knowing Jesus in a personal way.

Our objectives for our marriage are to continually grow together by working on our communication skills and our negotiation skills. Our goals as a couple are to build up the marriage, to strengthen it as we strive to be friends for life. We want more than anything to love and cherish each other, to be kind to one another, and to provide an example of Christ's love to our sons, our friends, and our neighbors. And so we root for each other in our quest for self-esteem, our search for meaning and positive identities. We work together to make our dreams come true. We are partners in life together.

With God to guide us, with a common goal, and a commitment to stick together—through thick and thin—I am confident that Jim and I will grow old together. I have no doubt that we will continue to support each other and learn from each other. I have no doubt that we will be friends for life, together forever!

Part 2

Listening with Our Hearts

Being Friends for Life Means Moving Toward Understanding

Dear Lord,

Sometimes our words, thoughts, and needs can get all mixed up and confusing. At these times we pray and ask You to clear the air, heal our hearts, clear our eyes, and open our ears to what we need to see, hear, and understand from each other.

When we are blinded by doubt,
          give us faith to see.
When we are deafened by anger,
          give us love to hear.
When we are shackled by fear,
          give us courage to reach out with love.
When we have given in to harsh words,
          give us the humility to forgive each other.
When we are stifled by confusion,
          give us the wisdom to speak with
understanding.

Help us to talk to one another. Help us to listen to one another. Help us to understand one another.

Amen.

Let your speech always be with grace,
seasoned with salt, that you may know how
you ought to answer each one.

Colossians 4:6

9

Alternatives to Being a Nag

I pushed my loaded grocery cart through the well-stocked aisles. I looked everywhere for pimento. It wasn't in the pickles section or by the olives. So I looked by the spices. Why did they always have to hide these things? Not that I really needed the pimento, it's just that the recipe called for it. And I wasn't secure enough yet in my cooking abilities—or in my relationship—to leave the safety of a recipe.

Now that Jim and I were engaged, he was eating most of his dinners at my apartment. In my continued attempts to impress him, I spared no expense or effort in the meals I prepared for the man of my dreams. I felt a familiar gnawing in my heart, that undercurrent of anxiety that warns me that I am on a harmful track. The feeling was so faint, however, that it was almost imperceptible. I almost ignored it. *Why do I feel uneasy about these groceries?* I wondered as I tossed lettuce, pimentos (found them, finally!), potatoes, and sour cream in a vain attempt to keep up with the rubber conveyer belt.

Is it the fact that I'm spending money that I don't have? I asked myself as I added peanut butter and jelly to the booty. That bothered me a little, but it didn't account for the deeper worry I was feeling. I reached for the six-pack of beer that I was buying for Jim. It was not the first I had purchased for him.

It's just a part of his life, I had rationalized. *He doesn't get 'drunk' anymore, and there's certainly no harm in one or two beers every now and then. After all, Jesus drank wine. There's no difference between fermented ale and fermented grape juice, is there?*

I had heard all of the arguments about alcoholic consumption from my Christian friends. Who was I to judge them? I had been raised in a home where alcohol was completely absent. Consequently, it was not a part of my life. Sure, I had tried it one night, visiting New York City with my friends, but I rejected it wholeheartedly with the first dizzy, giddy, out-of-control feelings. It was not for me!

I shouldn't make harsh, restrictive, legalistic requests of Jim. If he can handle a beer every now and then, who am I to make that decision for him? And so I had decided that I would buy beer for him. He liked it. It was no different than buying cola, I reasoned on.

I placed the six-pack by the cashier and watched the girl ring it up. I wrote out my check. I knew now why I was feeling anxious. I was not comfortable buying alcoholic beverages for the man I loved. I didn't feel right about bringing it into my home. I was about to marry him. Was this to be a part of my weekly routine? At that moment I knew I didn't want it to be.

The groceries weighed me down. They forced me to face something I had rationalized but wasn't at peace about. But how was I going to handle it? What could I do? If I asked Jim to stop drinking altogether, he might accuse me of being a nag. He might assent, but in his heart he could secretly resent me for imposing my ultra-conservative views on him. I didn't want to be a mother to him. I didn't want to tell him what I thought he should or should not do. I didn't want any authoritarian tug-of-wars polluting our relationship. I didn't want to control him.

Then an idea struck from out of the blue. *Don't say anything about it. Just pray about it.* Really? Not a bad idea. Instead of telling Jim about my feelings, I could talk to God about them. Let God work on Jim's heart. If it's God's idea and Jim's idea, then I won't ever be the focus of resentment. Would that work? Of course! Where was my faith, anyway?

So I followed up on the divine suggestion. I prayed about it, and I kept my mouth shut. That was the hardest part. It's hard to think that God can do things without my help. I tend to think that I have to interfere and initiate anything if it's going to get done.

Yet I was determined to do this God's way. I was excited to see what would happen. Every night before I went to sleep, I prayed, "Dear Lord, please work in Jim's heart to give up drinking altogether."

But occasionally Jim would go to the refrigerator, take out a beer, pour it into a frosted glass, and drink it down. I ignored it and concentrated on other important events in my life—like planning for the wedding.

One night, two weeks later, Jim put his arm around me on the couch. We had finished going over the wedding plans and were watching television. He reached over and turned the set off. "You know, Sheila, I've been thinking."

"Yes? What about?"

"I've been thinking that someday I'm going to be a father. You know, I don't think that seeing me drinking at home would be providing a good example for my children. They might see me drinking a beer now and then, or wine with dinner. Then they might think it's okay to drink. In my experience, that's how drinking begins, and drinking anything at all can turn into real problems. I have decided that I'm not going to drink anything with alcohol in it, ever again."

Wow! I couldn't believe my ears. And yet I could, for God had given me a lot of peace about this. In my heart of hearts I knew that God was going to be the One to tell Jim's heart. He had said as much in the grocery store. All I had to do was pray, not saying anything about it.

Jim was good as his word. We've never had alcohol in our home, and he has always politely refused wherever we have gone. For us, alcohol was something that we felt interfered with our lives and with our Christian walk. It was something that we chose to turn away from. And the decision was Jim's, not mine. I had no control over it, and I didn't have to worry about controlling whether or not Jim stuck to his decision. I have no doubt that this was the underlying reason that he has been so determined to keep his word. It was a pact between him and God. That's just the way I like it.

I could have told Jim kindly that I wasn't comfortable buying beer for him. I believe that God showed me a better way. It's a very simple way—letting God be in charge. But it's a difficult way, sometimes, at least for me. I wish I could say that I have always heeded His advice. But alas, my mouth often gets ahead of me. Unfortunately, I have frequently given in to the urge to speak my mind when it would have been better left unsaid. Do I always have to have the last word? Do I always have to be the one to instigate change? Do I always have to voice my opinion? Do I always have to be in charge?

Maybe I should learn to pray about it more, like I did when I was a tender, young fiancé. Maybe I should let God work on Jim's heart and mind my own business. Maybe that is the loving way. Maybe that's a more respectful way. Maybe that is the better way. Maybe that's God's way.

10

Men and Women— Appreciating the Differences

Women! Who can understand them? I certainly couldn't! In my active bachelor life, before I established my personal relationship with Christ, I had had a somewhat difficult time establishing and maintaining an ongoing and mutually beneficial relationship with any one female. It occurs to me now that those two things were *not* unrelated.

My quest was always to be seen with the most beautiful girls imaginable. I had the perception that fabulously beautiful women (definitely *plural!*) had to be my companions. I always felt that if I could be seen with a beautiful girl, then I would be admired, respected, and looked up to by my peers. Truthfully, I was not as interested in a relationship with a woman as I was with the status of being seen with her beauty.

Then I met Jesus Christ. My life changed. As a new Christian and through the guiding of the Holy Spirit, I began to tap into the tremendous reserves of Christian fellowship that surrounded me in the environment of my job and my new church. One day I found myself discussing my female relationships with a man I never would have dreamed could have impacted my life on the topic—the gray-haired Carl Wallace, a charming colleague who was instrumental in shaping my new walk with Christ.

I believe that only Jesus could create a relationship between a twenty-eight-year-old single man and a sixty-five-year-old married man to discuss the opposite sex! But thank goodness He did. Carl introduced me to a book written by Dan Benson, entitled *The Total Man*. Reading this book, written by a devoted, Christ-centered man, opened my eyes to new perspectives in the matter of my relating to women. Dan stressed that women are emotionally different from men, especially in the way they react or respond to given situations.

He pointed out that women tend to be far more sensitive to their surroundings and situations than do men. A man can slough off what a woman takes personally and carries with her at a deep level. Up until I read this book, I had frequently become angry with a female companion for acting in what I was learning now to be a typically sensitive "female" manner. I resented it when a girlfriend exhibited feelings and/or hurts that got in the way of a fun party time. I was terribly upset when a date would ruin an evening or an outing by complicating everything with her intense emotional reactions.

As a result, I had often found myself angry and sarcastic. When a female friend expressed to me some sensitivities about our relationship or a given situation, I tended to be verbally hurtful, to put her down. In fact, I had been known to literally abandon a date when and if the hassles jeopardized the "fun times." It never occurred to me that men and women are tremendously different in their emotional make-up. Not that I would have cared. I wasn't really interested in the emotional make-up of my female companions. In all honesty, I wasn't interested in feelings anyway. It was simply, and primarily, a physical attraction. "No emotional ties" was my unspoken motto.

God's timing *is* remarkable as I found myself reading Dan's book only weeks before my first date with Sheila. The ideas expressed in the pages of his book literally made all the difference in my relationship with Sheila. I still didn't understand her. But for the first time in my life, I was willing and I was trying.

I got a chance to put Dan's methods to the test shortly after Sheila and I became engaged. We were involved in planning our wedding. In my opinion, that is one of the single greatest challenges any couple can ever hope to survive! One evening Sheila became very emotionally distraught over a situation.

We were planning our engagement party. We wanted to have a sit-down dinner party and invite our closest friends who would most likely make up the eventual wedding party. We discussed the location—her parents' home. Great! We agreed. Their dining room table at the time was too small for the number of guests we hoped to invite. No problem. I reasoned that we could just move out the table for the evening and rent a larger table for the evening. Easy, or so I thought.

"My dad won't like it," she said.

"What do you mean?" I asked. I'd always known her father to be flexible in the respect that I've always seen him give priority to people over things.

"That table was Grandma's, and he won't want to move it."

I was *positive* she was wrong. And the ensuing conversational exchange escalated to a full-scale disagreement, tears (hers) and all. I could not imagine why she was so concerned over what I considered to be such a trivial thing. And now she was allowing it to spoil such a nice evening for us.

My old reactions began to rear up. But before they got out of control, I remembered Dan's book which suggested that instead of getting upset, yelling and screaming or clamming up and only making the situation worse, I take the approach of being gentle and understanding.

The idea was to sit down with her and try to gently talk it through.

Every ounce of me wanted to lash out, "Why are you ruining our evening like this with your unreasonable attention to such a petty, minor concern?"

But instead, as Sheila sat on an outdoor stairway with her head in her hands crying, I sat down beside her and put my arm around her. I gave up debating within myself whether or not it was right or wrong for her to be crying or concerned over the issue. Rather I just comforted her, I stroked her neck, stroked her back, kept my arm around her and said, "Sweetheart, I know you're upset and I'm sorry. Is there anything I can do to help?"

Pow! Her tension eased. I sensed it! I could tell that my gentleness had helped her. Treating her gently didn't make the situation any less upsetting to her. But it had shown me how to move through challenging moments without lashing out at the woman I loved and adored. It soothed and healed her emotional trauma to feel my sensitivity in reaction to hers, my gentle touch rather than harsh condemnation of her actions.

I'll admit that it is not easy for me to set my anger aside. I still get angry with Sheila at times and I try to remember to act in a gentle, understanding fashion. It's hard work and not part of my nature, but as far as I am concerned we committed ourselves to a lifetime of working these things out.

Interestingly, years later we saw a Gary Smalley tape. He was talking about the ability of one partner to "open their partner's spirit" when they have hurt the one they love. I watched Sheila through that tape and when it was over she said, "You know, Jim, I have to tell you, you are really good at 'opening up my spirit' after you've closed it. I really appreciate the gentle way you approach me and get me to turn back to you and open up myself to you again."

I'm certainly no marriage counselor. But I do believe that we men tend to have an ongoing problem in our inability to recognize God's greatest gift to us—our wives—and appreciate the fact that they are opposite from us for wonderful reasons! Too many couples find their differences a rub rather than an exciting opportunity to build and strengthen one another, to give support and to receive it, reacting and interacting with each other.

Male and female are just that, thank God; interlocking pieces of a puzzle that fit together as one, binding us together—forever!

11

More TNT

I love to aid in the classroom, so much that today I am working on getting my teaching credentials as well as my master's degree in education. The classes I am required to take all involve hours of field work, getting my feet wet by observing in classrooms.

One day, while I was wandering around one of the classrooms where I was observing, I noticed a mini-poster taped to the side of a tall file cabinet. It struck me immediately as sage advice and worthy of remembering. It said:

COMMUNICATION:
SAY WHAT YOU NEED.
SAY WHAT YOU WANT.

That night, after putting the children to bed, I looked around for Jim. I couldn't find him. He had retreated to his safe spot in the garage. I felt an ache, a fear that our relationship was going through a lonely spell. Even though we have committed time to each other, there are times when we don't connect. This was one of those times. Jim had been distant, and I suspected from past experience that he was feeling neglected. I knew that's how I was feeling. My school demands had crowded into the evening hours. The boys were having a rough year in school. I found myself working with them on their homework in the evenings. Nicky, our youngest had been sick—a lot.

I remembered the poster I had seen that day at school. I thought, *Okay. Here goes nothing.* I went out to the garage determined to communicate with my husband. I opened the door and saw that he was busy washing the car. I should have offered to help him with the car. I should have tried to talk to him, but because I tend to react in typical rabbit fashion to any confrontation, I lost my nerve and retreated back into the house.

Two hours later Jim emerged from the garage. As he was washing up I decided to try one more time. "Jim, can we talk?"

"What about?"

"Well . . . I . . . just think we need to . . . talk more." (*Why is this so difficult? This is my husband. What am I afraid of?*)

"Well, you know what happens when we talk about the household. You get mad. You cry. And that's the end of that," he said.

I burst into tears and fled upstairs.

Jim followed me. "I guess you're going to cry whether we talk or not. So we might as well talk," he said.

I turned on him, fire in my heart. "How dare you! How dare you say that we can't talk! I know I'm emotional. I know I'm sensitive! I can't help it. It's just the way I am. Besides, we'd be able to talk if you wouldn't always be so quick to fix things."

"Fix things? What does talking have to do with fixing things?" he asked.

"You always feel like you have to be able to fix everything! You try to fix my life the way you fix your cars.

I don't want to be fixed. I want you to have faith in me that I can fix some of my stuff myself," I responded.

"Well, if you don't want me to fix it for you, then what *do* you want from me?"

"I just want you to understand me," I pleaded.

"I'm trying. Believe me, I'm trying!"

"I just want to talk. About the weather. About the day. About me. About you. I want to tell you about my trials and tribulations without having you jump in with a suggestion for a better way. I just want you to say something like, 'You sound frustrated today,' or 'What an overwhelming feeling that must be.'"

Jim glared back at me. He gave absolutely no reply. Instead he walked out of the room.

I locked myself in the room and I cried.

Eventually, I remembered that I had a load of laundry in the wash. I had no choice but to go downstairs and put those clothes in the dryer. Otherwise, the boys would have wet jeans for school the next day.

Jim was in the laundry room. He watched me as I put the clothes away. I carefully walked around him so I wouldn't accidentally brush up against him. I kept my eyes lowered, so I wouldn't see his laughing blue eyes. Jim has this annoying strategy of making me laugh after we've had a fight. It always works, and I wasn't ready to forgive him—yet. I wanted to be sure he heard me first.

I hurled wet blue jeans from the washer into the dryer. Jim watched me. "I'm sorry," he said softly.

"For what? You didn't do anything," I lashed back.

"I've just been thinking about what you said. I realize now that you *just* want to talk. I have always thought you were asking for help, for advice. I see now you just want someone to tell your problems to. I will try to listen more to what you are saying and not fix everything for you. I love you."

"Well, I do need you to talk to me." (While I was at it, I decided to go for the grand prize.) I added, "I also need you to touch me more." When his eyes lit up with a devilish smile, I quickly added, "I mean I need touches that aren't just sexual advances."

He looked disappointed. I explained, "It means a lot to me when you hold my hand, give me a hug before you leave for work, tussle my hair, tickle me, cuddle with me, not because you want something from me, just to say you love me."

It worked! I said what I wanted and I said what I needed. I wanted and needed more TNT, more touching 'n talking. I knew I needed Jim to talk to me more. I knew that I was feeling lonely for him. I also knew that he was frustrated with our attempts at talk. Perhaps we could learn to communicate better. Maybe we could talk more.

I also had to tell him that I wanted more touches—more cuddling, more playful contact. What I needed from Jim were touches that communicated tenderness and love, touches that build bridges and bind. Touches that embrace and lead to intimacy, that keep our hearts woven together—forever.

That difficult conversation was a breakthrough in our quest to understand each other. Jim is a kind and sensitive man. He has really worked at listening to me. He heard me say that I need him to listen and understand more than I need him to solve my problems. To this day, when I complain about a difficult day, I can see Jim struggle to refrain from offering helpful advice. It's not easy for him, but he's trying. He has even said, "I know you don't want me to *help* you. But, I'm still not sure how I'm supposed to react here."

"What did you hear me say?" I respond.

Most of the time Jim tells me with clarity and insight how and why my day was frustrating for me. At those times I feel understood. I feel the heart connection with him. I'm no longer alone. I have a friend who cares and shares my life with me, and I have no doubt that we will be friends for life as long as we continue in our quest for understanding.

12

Too Late? Too Old? To Be a Hero

Some of my fondest childhood memories revolve around a handsome tall man in a freshly pressed U.S. Air Force uniform—my dad. I remember one day in the fourth grade playing softball at recess. Across the vast expanse of the crowded playground, I spotted this tall, handsome man coming my way, dressed in his great-looking uniform. I was so proud that he was my dad! I was sure he had spotted me among all those other children. I ached to be at bat so I could hit a home run for him.

Another time, I recall standing in the payroll line with him on base at the club. Hundreds of Air Force men, all in uniform. They all looked so tall and impressive to me. They'd ask, "What are you going to be when you grow up?"

"He'll fly the big boys," my dad would say while I shyly hugged his leg.

Big Boys were bombers, huge airplanes. I loved machines then, and still love them now. Airplanes, cars, boats, trains. I knew one thing for certain when I was very young. I knew that I was going to be in the Air Force when

I grew up, just like my dad. And, unlike him, *I* was going to fly the Big Boys.

As I grew older, all through high school, I always intended and assumed that I would serve in some branch of our U.S. armed forces. But I never did. Even today I study and read about all sorts of military hardware. I never miss an open house at the local bases, and yet I never served.

Why not?

Somewhere in my college years I lost direction. Those were the days when our country was in the midst of the Vietnam War and the controversy that surrounded it. One day in my freshman speech class, I was instructed to participate in a debate. I was assigned to debate in favor of America's involvement in Vietnam. Not a popular position at the time, but it was my assignment.

As I prepared for my debate, I studied the issues. The details of my research only bore out what my heart had already told me. A small democracy was under attack from a communist neighbor who had a huge, strong, big brother helping out. America's position to help made perfect sense to me, and my debating comments reflected my true feelings.

By 1970 and '71, when I reached my junior and senior years in college, the war and the issue had escalated. Students were shot at Kent State. Huge protest rallies took place on my campus. Students organized themselves to go into the surrounding neighborhood, knocking on doors, seeking support by signing petitions to end the war.

I joined in. My hair was growing long. I wore granny glasses. Sometimes I wore sandals. Mostly, I went barefoot. "Hippie" was the term anybody over thirty would have called me. I have never been a vocal person, so when we knocked on the first door, I let my protesting partner take charge.

"We're here today to enlist your support to stop the war in Vietnam. Will you sign?" she said.

"No!" said the lady at the door.

What now? I thought as I waited for my vocal female companion to respond. But instead she looked at *me!* I felt the pressure to say *something.* I didn't like the feeling. I wasn't sure where I stood on the issue. I was on the fence. So I made some weak response.

I tried to take the protesters' point of view. "They just want to grow their rice. They don't care what government they have," I said.

I was embarrassed. I had come along because I didn't know how to say no. I was on a huge campus. I was lonely. I wanted friends, companionship, so I went along on this door-knocking crusade. I knew I was out of my element. So did my partner. We quit. I went home. I felt confused. Unfocused. Why did I lack this direction? Why was I sitting on the fence?

All of this took place just over twenty years ago. Recently I passed a street corner with three of my sons in the car. Several people were there, crowded shoulder to shoulder, shouting and singing Lee Greenwood's song, "God Bless the U.S.A." They were enthusiastically vocalizing their support of our troops in the Persian Gulf. I saw their flags, their yellow ribbons. I heard the voices and absorbed the emotion. I started to cry.

"What's wrong, Dad?" Jason asked.

I explained to him. "You can never undo a bad decision," I said. And I told him of my fence-straddling during the peak service years of my life.

He thought briefly, and then my ten-year-old said, "Dad, go to the Gulf and serve!"

"Jason," I retorted, "I'm forty-two years old. They don't want me now, and besides that, God has blessed me with other priorities now. Three of them are in this car with me."

"You can never reverse a bad decision," I continued, and I told them about my dad and how proud I had been of him, my hero.

I was troubled by my encounter with the patriots on the street corner and my boys. I felt that I had let my boys, my country, my father, and myself down. That night I told Sheila about it. I said, "Am I too old to be a hero? Is it too late to set the record straight? Is there something noble and heroic I can still do with my life?"

Sheila looked me steadily in the eyes and said, "Oh, Jim, but you are a hero—to me and to your sons. You are a hero when you kneel with them by their beds at night. You are a hero to me when you come home to us each night. You are a hero when you play catch with your boys in the backyard. You are a hero when you come to us with tears in your eyes and say, 'I love you, will you forgive me?' You are a hero to me where you comfort me when I'm overwhelmed, when you are sensitive to my needs, when you wrap your arms around me when I'm discouraged.

"You may never get the purple heart from the president of the United Sates, but you definitely receive the committed heart from me and your sons. You are made of the right stuff when it comes to being a father and a husband."

We all make mistakes. We all have shadows in our past that we wish we could erase and redo. Sheila understood my need to forgive myself for an old failure. Her love helped me have the courage to talk about this old wound, face it, and, in the process, grow beyond it. Her love taught me that it's never too late, we're never too old to reach out for love, understanding, and forgiveness.

13

My White Knight

God granted me the desires of my heart. He led me to the man of my dreams, the man who could treat me like a precious teacup. I found my white knight, my Lancelot!

When Jim suggested a day trip to the mountains, naturally I volunteered to pack a picnic lunch. We had been dating, not long—and I desperately wanted to impress him. I had no money left in my checking account, but that never stopped me. I took it for granted that the way to a man's heart was through his stomach. And I was determined to make sure Jim's stomach was totally happy and satisfied. If it meant frequent dips into the automatic checking guarantee, no matter. Fifty dollars here, twenty-five there, I took advantage of this instant loan. I figured it was good investment in my future.

I ran to the store and stocked up on all the wonderful foods I thought would tempt the man of my dreams—ingredients for fried chicken, potato salad, chocolate brownies, and more. I packed it with pride and served it with confidence on a blanket spread under a towering pine and a crystal blue sky.

Jim was not disappointed in my efforts. "This is delicious, Sheila! I love your cooking. It sure beats peanut-butter-and-jelly sandwiches and chicken pot pies."

"I'm glad you like it."

"How do you do it?" he asked. "I mean where do you get the money for all these fabulous meals? I know that it costs money to buy the ingredients."

"Oh, it's no problem." (Of course it *was* a problem. As anybody knows, you never borrow money to buy an irreplaceable item such as energy or food!)

"Well, I'm glad you like to cook for me. I love everything you make!"

That day passed quickly. We strolled through God's country and packed up for the long trip back down the mountain. The curving roads wound through the majestic mountains. A spectacular view awaited us around each bend. We talked and laughed as we snaked our way down the road back to the real world.

Jim made sure we left the picnic site early enough so I would not be late for a performance I had that night in a local civic production of *My Fair Lady*. We were nearly all the way down the mountain, when Jim stopped to refill his car with gasoline. I reached for my purse, but it wasn't there. I looked in the back seat, but no purse. I pushed down my panic with great difficulty. I poked my head out the window and said, "Jim, you didn't by any chance put my purse in the trunk, did you?"

He looked up at me alarmed, "No. Why, can't you find it?"

"No. I don't know where it is."

Jim jumped to my rescue. He looked in the trunk, under the seats, everywhere, but the purse was nowhere to be found. He looked at me bewildered and said, "I can't find it. There's no way it's in the car. I've searched every nook and cranny."

"You don't suppose I left it in that restaurant where we stopped for coffee?"

"You must have."

"Oh no! Now what am I going to do?" The restaurant was nearly an hour back up the mountain. I couldn't possibly ask him to drive me all the way back up the mountain. And yet, I had to get my purse back. It had my keys, my identification, my checkbook—with the overdrawn balance.

Like a knight in shining armor, Jim said, "We'll just drive back up the mountain and go get it. Come on."

Each man has his own way of displaying his masculine prowess. Jim expresses his masculinity behind the wheel of a car. He zoomed up and around the curves of that mountain with amazing skill and speed. He leaped out of the car and disappeared into the rustic restaurant. Moments later he reappeared, triumphant in the old wooden doorway, holding the purse victoriously over his head.

"Hooray!" I exclaimed. "Thank you! Thank you!"

In my heart I thought, "What a man!"

We made record time back down the mountain. No leisurely, scenic cruise this time. The tops of trees whizzed by in a blur as Jim expertly maneuvered the car back down the mountain road. He drove me directly to the theater where I rushed backstage, breathless, barely in time to get in costume and make-up.

I sat in front of a row of theater mirrors, throwing my costume and make-up on. One of my fellow cast members said, "You're late tonight, Sheila. Is everything all right?"

"Oh, it couldn't be better!" I exclaimed, and I radiantly told her about the man who so gallantly raced up and down the mountain to retrieve my purse for me. I added, "And he didn't even get mad at me for leaving it there. Have you ever heard of anyone so wonderful in all your life?"

"Humph!" my fellow thespian snorted. "It's obvious you're not married yet, no *married* man would ever drive up and down a mountain cheerfully just to get a purse!"

"Well, Jim would. He'll always be this wonderful!"

Of course, my friend was closer to the truth than I was. Our superhuman efforts to please each other permeated the courtship and our early days of marriage, but in time the efforts relaxed a little here and a little there. My efforts at creative cuisine these days are frequently hot dogs and chips. I grouse when Jim reminds me I forgot to put the pickles on the table. (He *never* eats hot dogs without pickles.) The carefully crafted table with matching napkins and napkin rings has frequently degenerated to a roll of paper towels thrown on at the last minute.

Gone are the days of knights and fair maidens. Gone are the herculean efforts to impress. We have passed the courtship stage of marriage. I have since learned that this is a phase we all go through. And in time, this phase gives way to other phases. This is as it should be. As we learn more about each other, and as we become more secure in our love, we no longer need to put on shows that are beyond our means. We can be ourselves . . . completely . . . freely.

I am glad that we have grown beyond the false impressive behavior, the subconscious manipulative treatment that is a natural by-product of this stage. However, as we move toward understanding, as we become more honest in our communication, we don't have to abandon the graciousness of the courtship phase. We can retain the kind language, the gentle manners, the tender, loving care even as we grow more comfortable with each other. I have seen that it is possible to do just that.

14

Contradictory? Or Complementary!

I drive down the driveway after a long day at the office. The first thing my eye sees is firewood all over the front yard *and* backyard. Some of our firewood is about three feet long and two inches thick (the perfect size for clubs, guns, and swords for our four boys).

I mutter to myself, "All the toys the boys have to have, and still they play with the firewood."

Next I see the bikes strewn all over. None are on their kickstands. I move them, plus the wagons and the tractors, out of the way so I can get to the garage. I step out of the car. My tool box is open *again*. Hammers are missing. Screwdrivers are gone!

Through the garage window I catch a glimpse of the patio table. Papers are blowing in the breeze. Colored felt-tip pens (missing their caps) are lying all around. I mutter some more to myself.

I walk into the house. Jigsaw puzzles—two of them—are scattered on the kitchen table. *Why work two puzzles at once?* I wonder silently. The television is on. It's *loud*. Nobody notices me dragging in. You couldn't hear a semi-truck above this television.

71

"Hello!" I mockingly shout. One or two heads turn. "Hi, Dad." Their heads turn back to the television. The others do not even acknowledge me. They're drugged by the television, *again.*

I reach for the volume button and punch it down several notches. Relief! "Where's your mother?" I can speak more softly now. My proximity to the television also puts me in a position to be viewed and acknowledged now by the others.

"I dunno, upstairs maybe," one responds.

Upstairs I go, wondering why I have to step over and around pillows, blankets, toys, shoes, and assorted stuff to get there. I'm used to some mess, but this night it was worse than usual.

"Sheila," my voice sounds snappy now. I'm starting to blame her for all this.

"Yes?" I hear her voice coming from the direction of our bathroom/dressing area. I round the corner and there she stands. "Hi, hon," she says and reaches out for a hug. I'm not as responsive as I know I should be. I rationalize to myself that I could have been more responsive before the firewood, bikes, toys, puzzles, blowing papers, felt-tip pens, television, blankets, and strewn toys.

She senses my hesitation. I suppose it's familiar to her now. She's been married to me for twelve years. "Sheila it really bugs me and concerns me for legitimate reasons that our boys are not learning to complete their cycles."

"Completing cycles" is a term I use to mean finish what you start before you start something new. As in when you're done with the puzzle, put it away. *Then* get out the felt-tip pens and paper to draw. When you're finished with one project, put the materials away *before* you go outside for a bike ride. When you're finished with your bike ride, stand your bike up (out of range of the sprinklers) before you begin your adventure with swords, clubs, and guns (firewood). And when you're done with the firewood, put it back in the wood pile before you go in and turn on the television. *Too loudly!*

My dissertation is familiar. I know it is. Everyone in the household has heard it *hundreds* of times. "Why don't you supervise these boys so they'll learn these lessons?" I ask Sheila again.

My logical, relatively organized mind cannot comprehend a mind that cannot relate to my own thought processes.

"I'm doing the best I can," she says.

I know she is. I would not have fallen in love with this precious gift of a godly woman if she had not possessed the same basic values as I. And she, conversely, shared the same convictions as I or she obviously would have called off the whole thing before the altar.

I don't want you to do the best you can, I think to myself, *I want you to do it my way.* I would never say this to her. Even I recognize the arrogance of such a remark.

"This television's off until the bikes, tractors, pens, paper, puzzles, pillows, blankets, firewood, and everything else is picked up and . . ."

"Put away!" The boys complete my sentence with me in unison as they drag themselves, slump shouldered, toward the various areas of disorder. My finger hits the television's power button for punctuation.

I confess to being the disciplinarian in our home. I feel strongly that I need to be firm in my conviction to bring some gentility into the lives of four little men who stubbornly resist civilization. Nevertheless, emotionally, I'm about as soft as they come. This paradox adds yet another twist to the wonder of balance and complexity of God's wonderful authorship.

I am a firm believer in discipline, yet too much discipline leads to strict legalism. Adolf Hitler was the master of legalism. Legalism and discipline must be balanced with grace. My wife leans toward this sphere. She is more relaxed than I am when it comes to discipline. But she realizes that too much of this can lead to chaos!

She has admitted that she is thankful when I come home to get things back into line, as long as I don't accomplish this like a marching storm trooper, which is a mistake I've made. With her support and God's, I'm working on this.

Sheila is a different person than I am. We are like the puzzles all over the kitchen table. We fit together magnificently to yield a happy, healthy home for our children. If we were identical, we could never hope to interlock as puzzle pieces, to complete the beauty of the picture and the accomplishment. We would probably drift apart.

It is only through our diverse lifestyles that we hope to give our children a balanced view of living. It is through our ongoing cooperation and loving flexibility with one another, husband to wife, that our children will learn forgiveness, love, citizenship, diplomacy, and positive compromise. (Never settle for negative compromise.)

The next morning I go to work, and the cycle starts again. It's a new day. The kids learn a way of life from their beloved mother. And they learn a complementary approach from me. Some might think that the end result would be confusion. But Sheila and I feel that it is just as important for them to watch the cooperation, love, and understanding that is being modeled by their mother and father. We believe that children are keen to sense harmony versus discord here. After all, we are their *entire* world.

Contradictory? Or Complementary!

Sheila and I are quick to acknowledge to each other our own strengths and weaknesses, our abilities and our shortcomings. Our children watch us as we work to accept the differences in our individual personalities, and bring two complementary lifestyles to one marriage, one family.

15

Some Things Are Better Left Unsaid

I couldn't believe how nervous I felt. I felt foolish for feeling these old familiar butterflies. It had been years since I had dealt with the churning stomach and the sweaty palms that went along with performing. I have played the piano for years and years. I am forty years old. I took my first piano lesson when I was seven. I have paid my dues; I have done my part in countless recitals. I am no stranger to nerves, the ominous silence of the audience, the fear, the dread of getting stuck, forgetting my place, not knowing where to go from here. I was sure that those moments were behind me.

They weren't. The choir teacher at the boys' school heard from my son that I could play the piano. "Is it true, Mrs. Coleman? Jason says you're absolutely wonderful!" she asked with big, excited, expectant eyes.

"Well, I have played in my day," I modestly affirmed. I refrained from reciting my résumé by heart and recounting the hours of music that I had participated in college, the vocalists that I had accompanied in competitions. I just nodded humbly and said, "Yes, I used to play. I still practice at home when time permits." (I didn't add that all-important point that time rarely permitted any-more.)

"Oh! I'm so glad I got a chance to talk to you. We need an accompanist for the spring choir festival. I've always wanted the school to participate. But I've never been able to accept the invitation because we have never had an ac-companist. Would you be willing to play for the choir?"

Oh! My heart twinged with an old familiar leap of joy. The call of music beckoned me. It sounded like so much fun. I hadn't realized how much I missed my music. I said, "Well, when is it?"

As she recited the complicated rehearsal and perfor-mance schedule, I found that I wasn't even listening. I had already made up my mind.

I was going to get to make music again with a choir. What fun! Then the music arrived. I flew to the piano to get acquainted with the sounds, the melodies, the rhythms. Hmmm. It was more difficult than I remembered. Was I really so out of practice?

I knew I could master the tricky upbeats. I knew I could get that weak fourth finger back in shape so that I wouldn't miss that melody line *every* time! I did get bet-ter. I did get the rhythm figured out. I took my new re-sponsibility to heart and gave it my best. Finally the day of the first rehearsal came. This was just a rehearsal. So why was I so nervous? *I am just accompanying children,* I told myself. *I am not a soloist. I am just a background instrument.*

The choral room felt like a cold horror chamber. I re-alized with sickening clarity that this teacher had never heard me play. She had blindly believed a child's innocent, maybe exaggerated, faith in his mother. What would she think when she heard me? She would be too polite to tell me I wasn't good enough.

I managed to smile at this bright, cheery music teacher. The children began to filter in. One precocious young girl saw me sitting at the piano. "Hi, Mrs. Coleman! I didn't know you knew how to play the piano."

"Well, sometimes I'm not too sure I do," I laughed nervously. Why, oh, why had I agreed to this torture? Fun? What was I thinking? The teacher introduced me to the choir. "This is Jason's mom." I smiled with my mouth only. My eyes were filled with cold, hard fear. The director gave the downbeat, my fingers were shaking. To my horror I played the wrong keys. It sounded terrible! The girls looked at me. I could imagine what they were thinking. *An adult plays that badly?*

But the director only smiled. We continued. I played as badly as I have ever played. I was totally embarrassed. I felt like I should offer to withdraw, but that would be turning a bad experience into a closed door. I was not sure that I wanted to turn my back on music forever. So I kept silent. I kept going. I hung in there by the skin of my teeth. The director never once pointed out my mistakes.

She didn't need to tell me to go home and practice. Nobody had to tell me that I had made a mistake. Nobody had to criticize my playing for me. I could do that all on my own. I didn't need any help pointing out where I was weak and where I needed help. I knew. And I fixed it by myself.

Did that choir director realize what a gift she gave me when she refrained from pointing out my mistakes? Do we parents recognize the value of teaching our children to self-correct? Do we spouses understand how constructive it is to a relationship to keep our criticisms to ourselves?

"My husband says I complain too much," one of my friends told me one day. "He says I nag him. He asked me why I married him if I thought he was such a slob."

Like most couples, our attempts to "discuss" criticisms have rarely had positive results. When one of us has been criticizing, the other's shoulders slump, or the air gets tense. One spouse compares, corrects, complains. The recipient of all this "good advice" becomes hurt, bitter, distant. Barriers go up. We go back two steps instead of going forward. We grow further apart, rather than closer together.

Jim and I are really working to implement this self-correction approach in our home. It is not easy breaking old habits. We continue to point out things we do not appreciate in the other, but we are getting better at refraining. We are searching for alternative approaches, more positive methods. We ask questions like, "You seem unhappy with how the family budget turned out. Is there something we could do differently that would help?" Or, "You sound frustrated with your schedule these days. Is there something I can do to relieve the pressure?" Or, "You have been giving yourself to everyone else, what are you doing for yourself these days?"

We have discovered that when we ask questions, rather than shooting out with helpful suggestions, we send the unspoken message that we have faith that the other person is capable. We give each other the freedom to discover our own solutions to our problems, because we believe that this is where real growth and learning occur.

The Bible sums it up beautifully: "Love believes the best." It doesn't point out the worst. As friends, as lovers, as spouses, Jim and I draw closer together when we refrain from criticism, when we ask questions rooted in respect, and when we point out positive aspects. In the process, we build each other up and move even closer toward understanding.

16

Important Clues

Preadolescence hit a lot sooner than I had imagined! Eleven going on nineteen. Ambivalent. Sassy and sullen on one day. Sweet and sensitive on other days. Jason works hard to be a cool adolescent. Just don't let anyone see that he's with his mother and father. At other times, this whole business of growing up terrifies him. He wants to be a baby again. He sits on my lap—in public! He lifts up the back of his shirt and says, "Scratch!" Like all of my boys, Jason loves to have me scratch his back.

Some educators have pointed out that these preteens are caught in the middle, stuck in an uncomfortable twilight zone between childhood and young adult status. The transition is rarely smooth. In shaping their new identity, they test the boundaries, even try to get rid of them. As parents, we can all expect confusion and anger. These preteens are looking for more independence, more power, and more choices. And they're afraid of the responsibility such additional freedom brings. It's no wonder these are the beginnings of rocky times.

I couldn't believe that we were already entering the phase, and frankly it caught me off guard. I wasn't expecting this to hit until junior high. This was only fifth grade, for heaven's sake. But I could tell that Jason was having a rough time living with himself and with the high expectations of his teachers and his parents.

I found that I was losing my temper with him frequently, almost daily. His father was also angry at him a lot. Then I heard him repeat what his teachers had said to him. They were always mad at him, he told me. When I called to confer with the teachers, I discovered that they were unhappy with his attitude at school.

I worried. What had happened to my fun-loving, impish, elfin child? It had been a long time since I had seen him smile. When I dropped him off at school, he walked with stooped shoulders, chin dragging on the ground. Life had become a burden—at such a young age. It made my heart break.

Then I read a book called, *Cooperative Discipline*, by Linda Albert (American Guidance Service, Inc., 1990). In this book she said that all children have three basic needs: to *connect*, to *contribute*, to feel *capable*. Children's behavior is an attempt to satisfy one of those needs. Sometimes, due to lack of positive behavior models in the home, children will learn destructive behaviors. For example, in an attempt to connect, to reach out, a toddler will pinch another toddler. This toddler isn't being mean. It's just his young, crude, and ineffective attempt to reach out to connect with another person. If that toddler learns more positive ways to reach out, he will eventually abandon this ineffective strategy.

Linda Albert went on to explain that children who misbehave have four goals: attention, power, revenge, and avoidance of failure. We adults, we parents can identify the goal of their misbehavior or their root emotional need by listening to our responses. If we feel irritation with a child, then that child probably needs attention. If we feel anger or fear for a child, then that child needs more power, more choices in his or her life. If we feel dislike for a child, that youngster probably is feeling revengeful. If we are concerned for our children, then they need a more positive self-image.

This book was another answer to my prayers. If I could identify what my children needed, then I could concentrate on guiding them toward positive steps to fulfilling their needs. I could focus on the root need, rather than getting caught up in the surface emotional traps.

I listened to my feelings. Jason was making me mad. He was making his father mad. He was making his teachers mad. According to the concepts outlined by Linda Albert, Jason needed more power in his life. Instead of getting angry at Jason, I could talk to him about what's going on at home and at school. Does he need more freedom? Have we, his parents, been too restrictive? Does he need to be making more choices? Does he need more control over his life?

Jason confirmed that I was headed in the right direction. Jim and I felt that there were areas where we could loosen the reins. We made a change in his school. We included Jason in the search and the decision for a less oppressive educational environment. Overnight Jason regained the bounce in his step, the sparkle in his eyes. I cried with joy as I saw the joy return to the life of a child I had thought I was losing. I shudder to think what would have happened if we had not listened to our reactions, if we hadn't freed ourselves from the surface battle that Jason was trying to wage.

This method of paying attention to important clues works for me. It allows me to see my loved ones with x-ray vision. I can see beyond the surface smoke screens to the root need. When I find myself getting angry at a child, or irritated, or concerned, I stop and remind myself that these are signals I need to heed but not get trapped by.

If it works for children, can it work for spouses? Do adults have the same needs? Do we spouses have the need to connect? To contribute? To feel capable? The answer leaps out, Yes! Yes! Yes!

There is no question I need to connect with Jim. I need to feel that I belong to him. Sometimes I am too afraid to reach out. Or I am not sure how to make the first step. Sometimes, in my fears I resort to childish strategies, and my attempts have less than positive results.

I need to feel that I can contribute to the marriage, the home, the family. Likewise, I know that I need to feel capable. I long to be a capable wife, a capable housekeeper, a capable lover, and a capable friend to my husband. I also need to feel capable in my work, in my writing, and in my teaching. My self-esteem is crucial to my relationship with Jim.

We never outgrow them. I knew the three C's applied to me. What about spouses? If I heeded my reactions to Jim, could I better identify what he needs? Could I be a more understanding wife? Would I be freed from being trapped by surface actions and reactions?

I decided to give it a try. Jim didn't irritate me. So I didn't feel that he needed attention. He didn't really make me angry. So I didn't feel that he needed more choices or freedom in our relationship. I definitely liked him, so I didn't feel that revenge was a problem. But I had felt concerned for him. I had worried about him. I had longed to make him happy. Could it be that Jim needed to value himself more? Did he need to feel more capable? Did he need to feel that he could contribute to our marriage? To our family? To the work of God?

This, then, was my clue, my road sign. It was the first place to explore. And as I recalled conversations, I remembered phrases like "I want to make a difference." I now knew where to look, what to watch for. It was the first step toward understanding my best friend. It was the beginning of my being sensitive to Jim's real needs.

It's amazing what happens every time I stop and think of my loved ones and ask myself these questions. When I listen to my reactions and track back to the actions that prompted them and the needs that launched the actions, I find myself focusing, wondering, thinking, and analyzing the other person. What does he need?

In the process, I shift my focus away from myself to the other person. I begin to care about Jim and what he needs, rather than being wrapped up in my own troubles. I reach out with love and understanding. No wonder it works!

We couples can listen to our responses to each other and learn what our spouse needs. Does your spouse make you angry? Maybe he or she needs to feel that there are more choices and freedom in life. Does your spouse irritate you? Maybe he or she needs more attention. Do you dislike your spouse? Maybe your spouse feels bitter and revengeful toward you. Maybe you need to work on discovering forgiveness for each other. Do you worry about your spouse? Are you concerned about him or her? Maybe he or she is suffering from a low self-esteem.

These road signs, these clues can give us a direction to explore together. They can clear away the smoke that clouds the issue. By identifying what our loved one needs, we can be more understanding. We don't have to make it all better. But we can be there to support our spouse and walk alongside him or her and make the journey together — forever!

17

Self-Esteem

"I'm sorry, but I'm making cookies at my grandma's house this Friday right."

Again? I thought, but I didn't say it.

I fumbled for words just to get off the phone so I could end this extremely uncomfortable conversation.

I was a senior in high school. The girl I had just asked out was a junior, and a pretty one, or at least I thought so.

It had taken all the nerve I could muster to call her and ask her. Now she was telling me, "I'm sorry, but I'm making cookies at my grandma's house this Friday night." This was the same *exact* refusal I had gotten when I had asked her out seven days before!

I had been naive enough the first time around to actually believe she was making cookies with Grandma. So, foolishly, I had called her again.

What a dope I was! Perhaps it was just as well, now that I think back on it. At the very least, her lack of creativity in using the same excuse with the same boy two weeks in a row told me something.

But at the time I was crushed. My self-esteem, for whatever reason, was not and has never been strong. Just to call this girl in the first place had taken nearly a whole semester of hellos and smiles, in the halls at school and in class, so she would know who I was when I finally built up enough courage to even dial her number.

Now here I was on the phone with my heart pounding like crazy. My mouth and brain barely were able to speak. And instead of getting the longed-for date, I was confronted with what I now knew was a feeble refusal— the same one as last week.

I was truly humiliated!

It seems like my entire dating experience in high school and college was checkered with very uncomfortable boy-girl confrontations. And now, even today, nearly thirty years later I feel the same heart-pounding sensations in many of my daily relationships with people.

Of course, God has blessed me greatly and gratefully with my wonderful wife. It's amazing how the human being can keep on trying and trying and trying again (in my case with dating) until a perfect match is made.

My self-confidence and self-esteem have never been better since my marriage to Sheila. I still carry scars, but Sheila has done wonders with and for me. One of the first things she changed about me after our wedding day was the way I dressed. "You're not wearing those pants with that shirt to the office are you?" she said the first morning back from our honeymoon.

"I've worn this shirt with these pants for months. You've liked the combination up until now, at least you never said anything otherwise," I responded.

"Let's see what we can do with your wardrobe," she replied.

She rearranged my shirt/pant combinations. She even chose, on her own, two new sport coats for me. I immediately heard feedback at the office.

"Jim, you look nice today . . . new clothes?" the receptionist said the first day I walked off the elevator dressed in one of the new coats, pants, and shirts my new bride had set out for me that morning.

I called her immediately. "Sheila, thank you. You can dress me from here on out."

And she has. For twelve years now, she has set out a coat, a tie, a shirt, and a pair of pants every morning. And I still get the nicest compliments!

The only reason I go along shopping with her is so she can hang the clothes on my body. She chooses it all! It's a tremendous benefit to me. I feel a tremendous confidence in my appearance now when I walk into a meeting, a luncheon, or any gathering.

This confidence came new to me with my marriage to Sheila. Often she chooses a coat or tie, or shirt that I would *never* have selected in a million years. I keep my mouth shut. I've learned to trust her judgment, her leadership in this area. She's better at it than I am. Sheila and I have not eliminated my struggle with my self-esteem, but we have strengthened my self-confidence.

Recently I read in Dr. Norman Vincent Peale's wonderful book, *This Incredible Century,* how he confessed to a lack of self-confidence quite early in his life. He relates how his father suggested that he "must conquer this problem, elstwise it will hinder you the rest of your life."

I read this passage with real interest. Here was a man who was the epitome of self-confidence, yet he confessed to a lack of self-esteem. Several times, in fact, throughout the book, Dr. Peale relates to his battles with this problem.

I'm fortunate enough to have met and worked with Dr. and Mrs. Peale over the years as they sat for a number of years on the board of directors for the Crystal Cathedral Ministries. I was speaking with Mrs. Peale one day on the phone and took the occasion to mention to her how much it meant to me to know that her husband had experienced sweaty palms, heart pounding, and all those other things that I know go along with a lack of self-confidence. I shared with her candidly that I also had the problem.

"Not you too!" was her short but loving response. "I've been in board meetings with you, Jim. Your reports and presentations always sparkle. You're not going to tell me now that you're intimidated and nervous during them, are you?"

"I'm shaking in my boots," I confessed sheepishly. I felt silly suddenly. I realized that I have ten fingers, ten toes, two ears, two eyes, a nose, and a mouth. I have no deformities. What do I have to be self-conscious about?

Mrs. Peale's voice interrupted my thoughts. "You and my husband!" she declared. "We'll make it a matter of prayer."

"Thank you," I managed to say.

I hung up the phone, somewhat mad and frustrated with myself for even bringing it up. But I must. I *must* keep bringing it up, especially with my closest friends and associates, and especially with my wife. I can't hide it. I can't put it in a closet and ignore it. I must keep it out in the open where my wife can hear my heart and encourage me.

"Jim, when you speak to groups of people you always are wonderful," Sheila has said. I can't hear enough of this. I ask her to go on. She does, and I hang on each word. "You're warm and honest in your presentations. Your integrity really comes through."

I really appreciated those last two sentences, including, "Your integrity really comes through."

I want my integrity to come through, after all, that's the important thing.

Keep trying. This is the secret. When you're faced with something to do that's extremely uncomfortable, that's all the more reason to do it! These are growing times. We must force ourselves forward sometimes or we will never advance.

God bless my wife for the positive force she has been in my life to help improve my self-esteem. I expect that, like Dr. Peale's, the problem will remain a distinct aspect of my personality as long as I live. My wife's great and gracious, gentle and wonderful way of encouraging me is a benefit of our relationship as husband and wife. It's my responsibility to return the favor.

18

Listening with Our Ears, Our Eyes, Our Heart

I had cried out to my Lord and my God who is able to do the impossible, yet I could not see that I was growing. I was not changing. I wasn't doing any better than when I had started. I had prayed for years and years, "Help me do it better, Lord." "Help me bring peace to a houseful of fighting boys." "Show me how to keep from losing my temper." "Help me to understand Jim." "Help me to communicate with him when he is silent."

Was God there? Was He hearing my prayers? My cries for help? I was trying with all my might, but I felt like I wasn't making any progress.

Then I found myself taking teaching methods classes to earn my credentials. They were a far cry from what I had expected. In addition to teaching us "future teachers" creative strategies and methods for teaching various subjects, the professors dedicated a great deal of class time to how to treat children. They discussed how to build up their self-confidence. How to treat them with respect. How to motivate them. How to discipline them. I was intrigued. As a mother who had been struggling in her parenting and in her marriage, I was gripped by the concepts I was hearing. They made so much sense. Were these new strategies the answers to the prayers I had prayed for so many years?

One night, our class focused on counseling skills. In the professor's opinion, this is a vital skill for teachers to acquire in their daily work with children. "The first lesson in counseling skills," she told us that night, "is learning how to listen."

Oh! This hit a nerve with me. I'm really good at talking. But my listening skills were really weak. The professor continued, "The responsibility of a good listener is just to listen and to let the other person know that you have heard. It is not your responsibility to give advice, to help, or to fix. It is just your role to understand. You can do that by paraphrasing back what you have heard the other person say. Now that sounds simple, doesn't it? But it's much more difficult than you can imagine."

Then she broke us up into pairs and had us practice our listening skills. It *was* hard! I found that my mind jumped ahead. I was busy thinking of a response, a bit of helpful advice, or a defensive retort, so that when it came time for me to paraphrase what my fellow student had told me, I found to my dismay that I couldn't. "Would you repeat that?" I asked sheepishly.

My mind was spinning as I drove home from class that night. There was so much wisdom in this approach to "helping." It reflected respect for the other person. How arrogant I had been to think that I could offer advice to everyone who talked to me. Sure it made me feel good. But how did it make the other person feel? How had I made my boys feel over the years, not to mention the love of my life, my friend and lover, my Jim?

Old habits are hard to break! I had a hard time paraphrasing. I still do. But the times when I tried it, it worked!

One day my eight-year-old Scotty was visibly upset. I asked him what was bothering him. He burst out angrily, "You never pay any attention to me. You give Nicky and Jason lots of attention, but you never notice me."

I pushed back the urge to defend myself, to remind him of the times when I had listened to him, of the sacrifices I had made for him, of the times I had made special trips to his school to support him. Instead I recalled the professor's words, "Don't judge or defend."

So I said with sincerity, "Are you saying you need me to notice you more, Scotty?"

"Yes," he replied. "I need you to listen to me."

"You need me to listen to you more?" (This felt stupid. I felt like a parrot. How could this possibly be of value?) But then I looked into Scotty's eyes. His anger had dissipated. His voice was calmer than it had been a few moments before. He began to talk to me straight from his heart. He was telling me important stuff here!

"Yes," he added. "I need you to listen to me with your eyes."

Oh! The light went on! I suddenly recalled and saw myself for the first time through Scotty's eyes. I had always listened to him while doing the dishes. I listened to him while driving him to school. I listened to him while ironing. When was the last time I listened to him with my eyes and with my heart as well as with my ears? When was the last time I gave him my undivided attention? I couldn't remember.

I was overwhelmed by this exchange. I had learned a vital piece of information that I needed as Scotty's mother. I had learned how hard it was to listen, but also how valuable it could be. I pulled out my notes from class and scanned them. "It is important for the listener to refrain from judging the feelings being expressed. Show them by eye contact that you are paying attention. Do not say more than absolutely necessary."

I was excited. *This works!* I thought. It was hard work, but I continued to practice it. It was hard getting over the feeling that I was stupidly repeating back what they had just said. But it seemed like the more closely I repeated their phrase the more satisfied they were with our conversation. And it was really difficult to keep from judging what they were saying to me. At times I paraphrased back, but I said it with a touch of sarcasm, hoping they would see how silly their words sounded. Wrong! That was not the way to listen. They clammed up.

Jim was the hardest to listen to. The first time I tried paraphrasing back to him, he heard the hesitation in my voice and said, "Don't get all psychological on me!"

Oops! I blew it again. But I was determined. I tried it a few more times, with a similar response. Nevertheless, I was encouraged by the headway I was making in communicating with the boys. They were talking to me about important feelings. I was learning a lot. I was sensing more peace in my home and I was getting a fresh perspective of my *response abilities* as a mother.

Then one date night, Jim and I were driving down to the beach. He had been quiet lately. He wouldn't talk to me about what was bothering him. As we drove in stifling silence, I fought the feelings of inadequacy that usually assail me when Jim clams up. When Jim is withdrawn, I tend to defend or judge his silence. I usually find myself thinking such thoughts as *It's all my fault*, or *He doesn't love me anymore*, or *He's acting like big baby*.

This time I reminded myself that it wasn't my responsibility to fix whatever was bothering him. It was not my position to judge him for his feelings. Rather, I could be his friend by listening with love, empathy, and respect.

I looked over at him. His silhouette looked so down-cast. "Is something bothering you tonight, Jim?"

"Oh, it's the same old stuff."

"Are you feeling hopeless, like you'll never resolve some of your frustrations?"

"Yes!" he declared. "It seems like I've been going over and over the same ground. I keep dealing with issues and they don't get any better."

I thought, *Oh, good! He hasn't accused me of being an amateur psychologist yet. Maybe this method of communicating will work for us yet.* I replied, "Do you feel like you're stuck?"

"Yes! I don't feel like I'm making any headway in my life. None of my dreams have come true. I haven't accomplished anything I had hoped I would."

"What did you hope to accomplish?"

Silence. I was afraid that I had pushed. I was afraid that Jim would clam up. It had been going so well. I had felt that we were really communicating. He was talking to me from his heart like Scotty had done. I waited and watched. This was hard for Jim. I could see him struggling, thinking. Finally he said, "I always thought that I would be a good father. That my children would follow my example. I thought I had leadership abilities, that I could influence my employees and motivate them."

We continued to talk heart to heart. Jim worked hard. I was proud of him. It wasn't easy for him to talk about these things, but he didn't give up, he didn't retreat; he kept talking and thinking about what he wanted and what he expected out of himself and others. We didn't discover a "cure" for his concerns, we didn't "fix" all his problems, but we talked, we communicated, and Jim felt better.

The next day he reached out and took my hand and said, "Thanks for talking to me last night, Sheila."

I smiled and said, "I was proud of you. I could tell it wasn't easy for you to talk about all those painful issues. But you hung in there."

Of course, I still talk more than I listen. I get tired, frustrated, overwrought. I get impatient with this method. It's a lot of work. It takes more time to listen than it does to lecture. I get pulled in five different directions just by the other people living in the same house! I have hollered as we're running out the door, late for school, "I don't have time to counsel you boys every morning!" I have let sarcasm strangle the respect. I have forgotten or ignored all of the ground rules—"to refrain from judging and defending."

But there are other times when I make the effort, and the effort pays off. I am working on breaking my bad habit of thinking I have all the answers. I am working on listening with all my heart and my eyes, to understand, to empathize, to care, to hear their hearts' concerns with love and respect.

Part 3

All Things Being Equal

Being Friends for Life Means Giving and Accepting Support

Dear Lord,

Life isn't always fair and neither is marriage. Sometimes I don't get treated the way I think I deserve. Sometimes I don't get the respect I think I deserve. Sometimes I get more work than I think I deserve. Keep me from keeping score, unless it's a record of all the good that we do for each other. Help us maintain equality and equilibrium as we work through the delicate process of keeping our lives in balance.

Show us when we need to hold on,
and when we need to let go,
when we need to give encouragement,
and when we need to accept support,
when we need to be firm in our convictions,
and when we need to relinquish control,
when we need to be dependent,
and when we need to stand on our own.

The scales may tip from side to side, the weight of the responsibilities may shift from time to time, the balance of the relationship may rise and fall according to the demands life throws at us. Nevertheless, we believe that You, Lord, will show us how we can encourage each other, support each other, and work together. As we share our tasks and our lives we know that our love will grow richer. Thank You, Lord, for showing us how.

Amen.

Two are better than one,
Because they have a good reward for their labor.
For if they fall, one will lift up his companion.
But woe to him who is alone when he falls,
For he has no one to help him up.

Ecclesiastes 4:9–10

19

Love Lifted Me

I proudly wrapped the last of the six cookies 'n cream pies and rearranged the freezer to make room for all of them. In the process I mentally rechecked my list. Fifteen pounds of hamburger? Check. Forty hamburger buns? Check. Ice cream pies? Check. Birthday candles? Check. Beans? I would make them first thing in the morning. Our guests wouldn't arrive until late in the afternoon. There would be plenty of time.

I knew that the combination Labor Day/birthday party was all in order. Nearly forty of Jim's family would be here to help celebrate the last days of summer and our son's eighth birthday. It's always a lot of work to get ready for this big family event. But I have to admit that I enjoy the planning and look forward to the company.

Bed felt good that night. Sleep flowed deep and wrapped me tight. Suddenly a faraway ringing phone intruded on the blackness. *Go away*, I thought dreamily. The ringing persisted. Finally, I realized that this was not a dream. I shot up in bed, looking at the clock—4:30 A.M. Something was wrong. "It's nothing," I said, trying to calm the fear that was trying to grip me. *It's probably a wrong number.* But it wasn't.

"Sheila?" It was my mother. My heart pounded wildly. Immediately I knew something must be wrong with Dad. He had left on an overseas mission just two days earlier. There's always a fear that his plane might not make its destination.

Mom's voice calmly broke through my wild thoughts. "I have bad news. It's your father. He's in Amsterdam. He's bleeding in his brain. He's in surgery now. He's in a coma."

I cried out, "What?!" Then, "Oh, help Mother, Jesus! Oh, dear Father in heaven!"

Mom said, "Sheila, I've relinquished your father to God. He belonged to God in the first place. He will always belong to God. He belongs to Him even now."

Jim, hearing my cries, rushed to my side. "What is it?" he asked. Alarm filled his eyes.

"It's my dad," I said, tears choking at the words. "He's bleeding in his brain. He's in a coma. He's in surgery right now."

"Oh no! Oh, Sheila!" he said. He wrapped me in his arms and cradled me like a baby. He gently rocked me back and forth as I cried and cried.

"What can I do to help you?" he asked with tears in his eyes.

"I would like to call the prayer chain."

Jim and I belong to a network of small groups at the Crystal Cathedral. Each group has its own prayer chain.

Jim looked at the clock. "It's 4:30 Labor Day morning. Everybody's sleeping," he said. "Do you want me to call them and wake them up or wait until 7:30?"

I thought of all the dear friends we have at the Crystal Cathedral. I knew that Dad had helped many of them find a belief in Christ. I said, "That might be too late. Please call them now."

"Okay," he said. He called the pastor of our class and a few others on our prayer chain. Each of them, in turn, called others and got our whole church praying. Then Jim held both my hands in his and prayed for Dad.

I have never needed my husband more. And I have never loved him more. He heard my heart's cry and responded. He reached out to the community of believers and asked them to join forces in prayer. I am eternally grateful. Later we learned that within a half hour, more than six hundred people had been awakened in the black of the morning, more than six hundred people dropped to their knees by their beds, more than six hundred people lifted my father up in prayer.

God heard those prayers. In the ensuing hours, we learned that Dad had emerged from surgery and was in stable condition. Praise the Lord! Then we learned that he was awakening from the anesthesia and was talking. Praise the Lord! Then we heard the doctor say that we could expect a full and complete recovery without side effects in approximately six weeks. Praise the Lord!

The doctor's initial news was so much better than we had expected. We had expected to lose Dad. At best, we feared that if he lived through the surgery he would be an invalid for life. We were so relieved that we celebrated by having the birthday party anyway. Jim's family came over and each and every one of them hugged me and told me they were praying for Dad. We sang happy birthday to Scotty. And I went to bed that night, weary but relieved and praising Jesus.

The reports that came that week from Amsterdam, however, varied from day to day, hour to hour. My spirits rose and fell accordingly. Through it all, Jim was there. One day I fell apart. Jim listened to me cry. I can't recall a single thing he said to me, but I will never forget the tender, sensitive care that he wrapped around me.

One week passed. Everyone was asking, "When will he come home?" I was asking the question myself. I knew that my brother could not stay in Amsterdam indefinitely. One of my sisters, Jeanne, lives in Hawaii with her two little girls. Her husband was already over in Amsterdam, and he needed to come home. My other sister, Carol, was in Oklahoma being fitted for a new prosthetic leg. My youngest sister, Gretchen, had a new baby. The longer Dad remained in Amsterdam, the more likely it would be that I would need to be the one to go over and help out.

My decision was made when we got the news that Dad would require a second surgery. Mother called with the news. "Your father looks and sounds really good. The CAT scan, however, indicates that there's another blood clot. The doctors say they have no choice but to operate again."

"When?"

"Tonight."

"Mom, you sound so weary."

"Oh, I'm holding up okay. But your brother's tired. He needs to return home."

"Then I'll come and take his place. I don't want you there alone."

"Really, Sheila? That would be wonderful."

I hung up the phone. What had I done? I had promised my mother I would fly to Amsterdam and be there with her and Dad for a week. But what about my commitment to my husband and my four small boys? I called Jim at work.

"Jim, Dad is going to have a second surgery."

"Oh, no!"

"I told Mom I would fly over and help her out."

"Of course. I understand. Don't worry about me and the boys. I'll take care of everything."

What a gift Jim gave me at that moment. He gave me the freedom to fly to my parents' side at their moment of greatest need. His love and understanding lifted me and allowed me to go half a world away at a moment's notice. I knew I could count on him. I knew I didn't have to worry about him or the boys. They would be all right until I got home. In the meantime, I could take Jim's love and extend it to my parents. I was able to hold Mom in my arms. I was able to embrace my father. I was given the chance to tell them things I would have waited too long to say. I had the chance to tell them over and over again, "I love you. I love you. I love you."

Those were priceless days alone with my parents. And I couldn't wait to get back home to my family, my boys, my husband. The flight home was uneventful. Mom and I watched over Dad like hawks, but he didn't need the attending doctor or nurse. He did fine. He was so excited to come home!

An ambulance met us at the plane and drove us to the hospital where Dad was to remain overnight for tests and observation. I knew that Jim would be waiting for me at the hospital. The ambulance got nearer and nearer. As it turned the corner, I saw a bank of television and newspaper cameras and reporters. And standing off to the side, away from the reporters, smiling from ear to ear was Jim. Oh, how good it was to see him. The door of the vehicle opened and I flew into his arms. We had made it home!

I had no doubt that Jesus placed Jim in my life for me to lean on during the difficult times. His sensitive care upheld me when I thought I was going to fall apart. His love, his tenderness, his understanding lifted me and carried me through one of the most difficult times in my life. He did everything just right. No one could ask for more!

20

Equality? Or Equilibrium?

"That's not fair! He has more than I do!"

How childish, I say to myself in exasperation as I measure every millimeter of spaghetti, weigh every ounce of chocolate cake, and cut jellybeans in two in my attempt to appease my little experts of inequalities.

My four boys have sharp eyes. They immediately spot uneven treatment, unequal attention, and especially unbalanced portions of food. I cannot remember a single meal where there was not some food left over. Our table is bountifully spread. There is no worry about having enough to go around. Yet my boys lunge at the platter like a sprinter leaps at the sound of the starting pistol. Amen. Bang! We're off and running!

Jim and I both get exasperated with this mysterious behavior. We could understand it if we were in the middle of a depression, if we were war refugees, or if we were suffering from malnutrition. But there is plenty. What are they afraid of? What is triggering this self-protective mechanism?

It's not just at the table. They keep careful tabs on what we spend on each of them. For boys who struggle with math papers designed to teach the addition and subtraction of money, they keep mental accounts that would put any local CPA to shame. "You spent more on him than on me!" "You owe me!"

More than money and food, the boys are painfully aware of each minute spent with the others. If I read for thirty minutes to one boy, I am expected to read for thirty minutes to each and every one of the boys. I love to read to my children before they go to bed. It is our favorite time together, one-on-one. But I don't like doing it to a stopwatch.

Life with our four boys is like living with a giant scale. The minute one side tips in favor of one or the other, the entire household literally screams at me, "Not fair! Not fair!"

Again, it is easy for us grown-ups, us mature adults to sniff, wring our hands, and proclaim, "What childish behavior!"

Is it? Do we ever outgrow our desire, our need for justice, for fairness, for equality? Perhaps we are not as conscious of our need for it as we were when we were children. Or perhaps it's just that we feel childish demanding our fair time. However, if we are really truthful with ourselves, we would have to admit how much it hurts when we are not treated fairly.

Inequality between the sexes has been a hot topic for nearly a century now. Suffragettes turned the battle of the sexes into a political debate that grinds on still today. Many men are afraid of women's lib proponents. And frequently, women are afraid to demand their rights for fear of being misunderstood.

Like little children, we adults are busy grabbing for what we can get, for fear we will lose out. In my opinion, fear is the root of all this perceived inequality, especially that found in marriages. There have been times when I was afraid to do and be all that Jim needed me to be. Why? Because I was afraid that I would lose my independence, my identity, my self-esteem. I was so afraid of what I would lose that I was unable to give Jim all he needed and wanted from me.

Likewise, Jim has had his own fears. I have heard him say that he has been afraid that I would neglect him, that I would devote my time and my energy to my boys, to my projects, until there was nothing left for him. He was afraid that he was going to lose out.

Such fears can kill a marriage. Such self-preservation can block intimacy. We know because we have fallen victims to these fears at times. In our attempt to get our fair share, we nearly lost what we wanted, and needed most—love.

Fortunately, our love has grown, our friendship has matured. Jim and I are more secure in our identities and self-concepts than we were when we first got married. We recognize our needs and we treat each other with equal respect, equal importance, equal love.

Life is in a constant state of fluctuation. We individuals who make up the living relationship are changing and growing. And as we change and grow, our needs waver. Some days I need more from Jim, and some days he needs more from me. If you looked at the scale in our house, I doubt that it would ever be in balance. The important thing is that it is not tipped at all times to one side. It bounces back and forth according to life's demands. We work at balancing our relationship, knowing that when we keep our needs in equilibrium, our love will be rooted in equality, free from fear.

21

I Need Help!

I'm sure God never intended me to go through my life alone. It seems pretty clear that His dream is for all of us to find love. And when we do, His intent for all of us is to have marriages that last. He wants all of us to be together forever. Through God's grace, that has only happened in my life because I was able to admit my needs to myself and to others. There have been many times in my life when I have had to be big enough to say, "I need help." Probably the most important time I ever uttered those words was before I married Sheila, when I was a wild and crazy single man, returning home from a wild weekend at Las Vegas. It seems like it might also be part of God's plan that we know how to call out for help before we commit to being married.

The noisy sound of the bus's diesel engine could not drown out the robust party sounds of my hearty friends coming from just the other side of the flimsy bathroom door. I had taken refuge inside the bus's restroom, which was a very small cubicle located at the back of the bus. The air was rank. Thank heaven for a small latchless window that flapped open and shut, open and shut. The fresh air fought with the diesel fumes in a vain attempt to ventilate the pint-sized john.

My friends and I were on our way home, and for the first time I noticed that I had begun to question our behavior—mine especially. Now, as the bus rolled down the highway, I looked into the bleary eyes that stared back at me from the mirror in that tiny restroom, and I wondered who it was I was looking at.

I had been working at the Garden Grove Community Church (now the Crystal Cathedral) for almost two years as a graphic artist. I had sat at the same table with its relatively well-known and popular pastor—Robert Schuller. When Dr. Schuller first hired me, he had received an anonymous phone call. "Did you know that the artist you just hired is an atheist?" the mysterious caller inquired.

"I can't think of a better place for him, than a church, can you?" Dr. Schuller had replied. It was this attitude of acceptance and love that attracted me to the people I worked with at the church. I had met Dr. Schuller's family. I had been welcomed with open arms onto his staff. I was surrounded each day at the office by people who called themselves Christians. They never questioned or condemned any part of my lifestyle.

Not that my lifestyle was all that unusual. All of my friends away from the church drank beer, wine, or hard liquor. All of us were in our early twenties, and drinking was the natural, acceptable, and almost necessary part of our social life in Newport Beach, California. Not that Newport was any different from any other place. From age twenty-three to my then age of twenty-five I had developed the habit of limiting activities to those that I was readily able to attend with an ice chest of beer, or a pint of liquor in my boot or pant leg. I didn't consider myself or my friends to be alcoholics at the time, but lately I had to wonder if the seeds of the disease had been sown.

As I finished rinsing my hands and face in the tiny bathroom sink, my eyes lifted once again to see the face in the mirror. My hands left my face, beads of water trickled down my forehead to my chin. I gazed motionlessly into the face in the mirror. I did not immediately reach for a paper towel. I simply stared.

For the first time I clearly saw him—with his bloodshot eyes. I knew myself to be a gentle person, far from tough. But the man in the mirror looked tough. Wild. Drunk.

"Jesus, I can't do this alone anymore." The words passed from the lips of the man in the mirror. They were spoken quietly, but I heard them. For some reason I wasn't shocked at what I heard. This was the first time in my life that I had addressed Jesus by His name and not merely used the name as an expletive.

My eyes closed briefly, almost as if in prayer. That tiny, smelly, noisy bathroom for a moment had become a still, quiet sanctuary . . . but only for a moment.

I quickly turned, reaching for the recessed door handle, unlocked it, pushed the door open, stepping back into the hopping and hollering, the cigarettes and the beer. I sat down among the brood. Opening another can of beer, I bummed a cigarette and swayed with the gentle rhythm of the bus that was rapidly carrying us in our bliss back to reality—our jobs, our responsibilities—all the things we had fled from the previous Friday evening.

What had the encounter with the man in the mirror meant? What did the prayerlike words mean? It didn't seem to matter at the time. But little did I know that I had asked the power of the living God to come into my life and change it. I had said, "I need help." Little did I know that my life would never be the same again.

My childlike prayer on that noisy bus was the turning point in my life. I admitted to God, to Jesus, that I couldn't do it on my own. God heard my prayer. Indeed, He knew my heart's needs before I verbalized them.

That was the beginning of my new life. Over the next few months I felt God redeem me. He worked on my life and cleaned up the mess I had made of it. He saved me and gave me a fresh start.

It all began with those three simple words, *I need help.* And even though God began a good work in me, it has been up to me to keep the good work going. He brought love into my life. He brought happiness and joy into my life. He brought purpose and meaning into my life. But that doesn't mean that life has been easy street since that day I met Jesus in the bus. I don't think a day goes by that I don't call to Him:

"I need help understanding Sheila."

"I need help understanding my kids."

"I need help understanding myself."

"I need help understanding how relationships work."

At times it has been hard to say, "I need help." For some reason I like to go it alone. I guess I don't like openly admitting that I can't fix my life and my relationships by myself. It's not manly to admit that I need others to help me––my wife, my pastor, my friends. Yet I have tried going it alone. And I found out the painful way that it's a dead-end road. I always pray that I'll never go that way again. There's a better way!

22

Like a Precious Teacup

Every one of us yearns to be loved, honored, and cherished. We have all longed for that special, intimate relationship with one person in which we are treated with respect and feel priceless and irreplaceable. There was a time in my life when I feared that such an emotionally fulfilling relationship would elude me forever, that I would never know the joy of being cherished by one man.

I threw myself into my job, working with the youth at the church, but it was far from the fulfillment I craved. I was usually able to push the empty feelings into the dark crevices of my mind, but occasionally they surfaced and overwhelmed me with a full-blown case of depression.

I did everything I could to keep my fears of eternal loneliness to myself. I would have died if anyone would have guessed how desperately I craved a loving, intimate relationship with a man. I wanted a husband and children—a family of my own.

One day, unable to hide the loneliness and pain, I poured out my feelings to my father. I remember it as if it were yesterday. The sun filtered through the hanging plants and bounced off the rose patterned teacups as my father and I sat in the breakfast nook. It might have been a magic moment, but I was unable to see or feel the beauty that surrounded me.

My father had sensed my loneliness, the emptiness that I had been struggling with lately. He reached across the table. Taking my hand, he said tenderly, "Sheila, what do you want out of life?"

I didn't answer immediately. Instead I looked around me and thought of the home I had been raised in. I watched my mother as she worked in the kitchen. I considered how my father had treated her in their marriage. My father cherished her! I wanted the same thing. I didn't want to go through life alone. I wanted to have that one essential friend who loved me more than any other person in the whole world.

Suddenly, all the pent-up hurt, fears, and loneliness came pouring forth as tears streamed down my cheeks. Through the tears I managed to say, "All I want is a man who will treat me like a precious gem, like a fine teacup!"

Dad's eyes filled with tears as he, too, shared my hurt and listened to my cry. In his heart he felt helpless. There was nothing he could do to help me with my heart's deepest need, except to pray. Which is, of course, quite a lot. He said, "Sheila, that is a noble dream. Every woman should have a person who will treat her as a precious gem. I'm going to pray that God will send you a man like that. Meanwhile, you pray that God will mold you into the woman that this wonderful man will need. I believe that when the *time* is right, and when *both of you* are right, God will answer our prayer."

So, I began to pray for my heart's desire, for a lifelong friend. I prayed for the man that God would bring into my life. I claimed the verse in Psalm 37: "Delight yourself also in the Lord, and He shall give you the desires of

115

your heart. Commit your way to the Lord . . . And He shall bring it to pass." Since I had committed my way to the Lord and because I had put Him and His work first in my life, I began to believe that the desire I had for a husband and a family was His desire for me. I prayed that He would fulfill the desire or take it away from me.

God heard my prayer. He heard my heart's plea for a lifelong friend. He gave me a man who treats me like a fine teacup—but not for five years after that morning I shared with my father. It took that long for Jim and me to grow into the people who could enter an intimate relationship with maturity. It took five years for us each to identify our values and needs and to discover our growing personal faith. We each had to develop an intimate relationship with Jesus Christ before we were ready to enter into a relationship with each other.

When I first met Jim, a long-haired artist, I never dreamed that we would be friends, much less that four years later we would date. Heaven forbid, and I wouldn't have believed that five years later we'd stand side by side, vowing to love, honor, and cherish each other—for the rest of our lives!

Jim has been as good as his word. He has faithfully kept his commitment to me. He loves me. He honors me. He cherishes me. I sense it in his tender glances. I hear it in the respect he expresses in our conversations. I see it in the common courtesies he extends. I feel it in the support he gives my dreams.

Jim loves me. Jim honors me. Jim cherishes me. Jim supports me. He calls me during the day to tell me he loves me. He sends flowers when I'm feeling overwhelmed. He brings me a cup of mocha. He hides greetings cards around the house or in the car.

And likewise, I love, honor, respect, and support Jim. I listen to him when he needs a listening ear. I work to keep the house comfortable for him. I make sure that there is always a pitcher of cold water on the table for him. And I put the boys to bed myself so he can have that time to practice his piano. Through all these deeds of love, we are giving and accepting support from each other.

Nevertheless, we are all human, and from time to time our relationship suffers from the sins of our humanity. We neglect each other. We hurt each other. We don't mean to, but sometimes we let the love tarnish, the honor whither and die, and the cherish fade. We take our precious love for granted. Like a delicate teacup, we neglect it and allow it to get dusty and dirty.

Because we have committed ourselves to treating each other with respect, we're both working at supporting each other. We're both looking for areas that need to be rebalanced. And when we encounter times when the relationship is unbalanced we make the effort to support each other and accept each other's support. We go to one another in love and say, "What can I do for you?" Or, "Would it help if I were to take the boys for the afternoon?"

In this way, we dust off the relationship. We discover the beauty that has been there all along, just waiting to be appreciated. And so we recognize once more that our spouse is a priceless heirloom, a precious teacup, a cherished friend—someone whom we will love, honor, and cherish—forever!

23

Can Wedlock Survive Deadlock?

It goes without saying that marriage is a give-and-take proposition. It is negotiation at its most challenging. It's difficult to arbitrate highly charged emotional issues such as feelings, wants, needs. To maneuver successfully through the minefields of a deadlock, wedlock requires love, respect, and a sense of fairness. When we have left out any of these perspectives, the deadlock has erupted into full-blown war.

To paraphrase Paul, "Love believes the best" (1 Cor. 13). When I feel that Jim loves me and wants the best for me, and believes the best about me, my defenses melt, my heart and my mind shift from a defensive mode to a co-operative alliance. That's when I am willing to hear his guidance, his concerns, his fears. Even when I don't agree with his concepts, or his requests, I can't argue with his *love*.

Respect is another important ingredient when we've approached the negotiation table in marriage. Both points of view are valid. We are both entitled to our opinions. We don't always have to agree, but we have to respect our partner and reflect that respect in our choice of words and attitudes.

Deadlock comes with wedlock. It's not the deadlock, or the disagreement that causes it, that reflects the health of a relationship. How does the couple resolve their differences? What strategies do they use for the delicate task of unraveling a deadlock and getting beyond it? This is the crucial issue. What we do when our wedlock runs into deadlock can make or break a marriage.

Early in our engagement, Jim and I had discussed our interpretation of the Bible verse, "Wives, submit to your own husbands" (Col. 3:18). We had decided that when push came to shove, when we ran into a deadlock, one of us had to have the final say. When we couldn't agree, I would bow to Jim's wishes. I had agreed wholeheartedly to this arrangement because I knew Jim loved me. I also firmly believed and trusted that God would guide me through Jim.

One night, in the midst of wedding preparations Jim asked casually, "Are you planning to work after we get married?"

"Of course." It never dawned on me to do anything but work at an office. I loved being at the office. Jim was at the office. Why would I want to stay home? There was so little for me to do there.

He got real quiet, like Jim does when he has something difficult to say. Finally he said, "I think you'll want to spend more time at home once we're married."

"Why?" I asked.

"Well, there will be more for you to do. I don't think the weekend will be enough time to get everything done you'll need to do, once we're married."

"Well, I suppose I could take an extra day and stay home one day a week."

"That's still not enough. I would like you to stay home two days a week."

My stomach knotted. I could tell that Jim felt very strongly about this. But I didn't feel that his request was at all necessary. I had always packed as much into my life as I could. I never had a minute to breathe. We were planning to move into a brand-new condominium. What in the world was I going to do for two whole days, *alone* in a condominium?

I gulped. I knew I had to tell Jim how I felt. "I really don't want to stay home two days a week," I said as I braced for his response.

"You may not realize it now, Sheila, but you will need two days at home. I am asking you to be home and make our condominium a home. I understand that you want to continue working. I think that three days a week at the office is all you'll be able to handle without getting overworked and overtired."

I had never expected this. I had been a free single girl for many years. I really struggled with the idea of having anyone—even the man I loved—tell me how to spend my days. I wasn't willing to give up my control, and my resolve stiffened as I said, "Please, Jim. Try to understand that I don't want to be home that much. I'll get lonely and bored."

He said, "What's wrong with staying home? I'm not locking you up in a cage. I love you. I think this will be good for you."

But I felt like I was being locked in a cage. I felt like someone was trying to strip away my freedom.

Jim quietly stuck to his position.

Suddenly, we were putting our agreement about how to handle deadlocks to the test. It had been easy for me to agree with the agreement. But now that we had run into a stubborn wall, I wondered what I had gotten myself into. I felt Jim was being unreasonable. I had communicated my position clearly. Jim knew where I stood. He didn't understand it or agree with it, but he heard my feelings on the subject. Nevertheless, he stuck to his original request and I knew that there was nothing more I could say. I could either accept his position, stick to my commitment to his leadership in the relationship, or call the whole thing off. We faced our first deadlock.

I looked at my husband-to-be. I heard him say, "I'm not locking you up in a cage." Even though it felt like a cage, I heard the love in the request. I saw the confusion in his eyes. Why is Sheila so reluctant to accept this most precious of gifts—the gift of time?

Little did he know how hard it was for me to be alone. He didn't know that I was afraid to slow down and look at myself too closely. But God knew. It was God's idea that I be home for two days a week. It was God's idea that I slow down long enough to hear Him talk to me. It was God's plan that I stop running away from myself.

I didn't understand the wisdom behind the request. On the contrary I wholeheartedly disagreed with it. I silently asked myself, Who is this guy imposing his wishes on me and my lifestyle? What right does he have?

Of course he had every right. My life was soon going to be his life as well. I was no longer going to be single. I was no longer making decisions alone. My calendar was no longer mine. It was ours. And in choosing to be a wife, in choosing a lifetime partner, I was relinquishing the right to think of myself first and foremost. It was time to consider someone else's needs as well as my own, and Jim was saying to me that he needed to have me home two days a week.

So I agreed. I gave my boss notice. I told her I would be willing to continue working for her, but I would only be available three days a week. I chose to stand behind the needs of our relationship, rather than what I thought were my rights. And to tell you the truth, I never, ever regretted it.

Yes, there were lonely days. Yes, there were boring days. But all those days—even the lonely and boring ones—were also growing days. For the first time in my life I had to look at myself and get to know myself. It was an invaluable time of self-discovery. I barely had time to get to know myself when the babies came, and came, and came, and came. Now I can't get enough time alone at home. I long for more of the peace and quiet I had when we first got married. I'd give anything for some of that precious gift of Jim's—the gift of time.

The longer Jim and I have been married, the fewer deadlocks we have encountered. Our negotiations are more successful. The differences are resolved more easily, with less conflict. Perhaps it's because the years have strengthened our *love*, they have cemented our *respect* for each other's abilities, they have taught us to be *fair*. We have found, much to our surprise, that it is possible to make love, not war, when wedlock runs into deadlock.

24

Life's Little Surprises

I love surprises. So you can just about imagine how curious I was when Sheila called me at the office and asked if I was available for *lunch . . . today!* Our first son, Jason, was in the midst of his "terrible" or "terrific" twos (depending on whether you're an optimist or a realist). Christopher, four months old, was recuperating from his bout with spinal meningitis. Any time alone with Sheila was precious, and this unexpected gift of time alone with her was a most pleasant surprise.

We met at our favorite restaurant. My curiosity about this impromptu meeting was heightened by a wrapped package I noticed under her arm as we met and kissed in the parking lot.

Sheila had never before given me a gift at lunch. *What's up?* I wondered. It wasn't our anniversary. I knew I hadn't forgotten that. It wasn't my birthday. I certainly wouldn't forget *that!* I poked the box and teased, "What's in there?"

"Never mind."

"Who's it for?"

"You."

"Me? Why? What's the occasion?"

"Oh, no occasion. It's just a little something I wanted to give you." We walked toward the door.

My curiosity was getting the better of me. What was in that box? Why had Sheila decided to give me a present? I imagined a new shirt. Sure that's what it was! She had seen a shirt at the store today and had gotten it for me.

"Is it a new shirt?" I watched her face closely for disappointment or a hint of striking at the truth. But she just smiled sweetly back at me and said, "You'll see."

I held the door as we entered the restaurant. "Well, I don't get it. What's the point? Why do I have to wait to open this present? Why can't I unwrap it now?"

"You'll get to open it when the time is right. Not a minute sooner."

The hostess led us to a nice booth. It felt great to anticipate this unexpected midday affair with my wife. The mysterious little package heightened my pleasure.

It's not big enough for a sweater. My mind silently examined the package for clues. *It's too light for a book,* I reasoned. *I can tell that by the way she handles it. It's not long and narrow, so it couldn't be a tie. What is it?*

Sheila, seated across from me, gave me that smile of hers one more time. Then she slid the present across the table. "Okay. You can open it now."

Oh boy! I tore off the paper, opened the box, and there, wrapped in tissue were . . . two little booties. Within a fraction of a second my mind raced. *Booties?! Are they Christopher's? Were they mine, a pair that my mother saved? Is this entire charade just a trip down memory lane?* Then I saw a slip of paper. Sheila's eyes were dancing, "Read it!" she urged.

The first test said no.
The second test said yes.
God's ideas are always best.

Oh! Oh! It all began to fall into place. The test. I had put the test out of my mind. I had laughed when she suggested she was pregnant—again! "We have two babies already!" I had protested.

She hadn't been satisfied. She had called the doctor, had a test, and the doctor had told her it was negative. She wasn't pregnant. I could have told her that. And said as much. "The first test said no," but "the second test said yes." What second test? I looked at the booties. I looked at Sheila's shimmering, dancing eyes. All I could say was, "Really?"

She nodded and said, "Yes. There's no doubt about it. We are going to have another baby!"

It may be hard to believe, but I can't tell you how full my heart felt. And what joy and excitement (and a twinge of nervousness) suddenly swept through me. Even though I would never have planned it this way. Never in a million years would I have had the courage. God's ideas are always best. I knew that. I knew that this was God's surprise baby for us. I reached across the table and took Sheila's hands in mine. "Boy! You really surprised me! I *never* would have guessed what was in that box! But no one has ever given me a more wonderful gift. Thank you, Sheila!"

Life is full of twists and turns. You think you have it all figured out and then wham! You get handed a surprise!

I like to know where I'm going. I like to plan my day. But sometimes life throws in a few changes, a few "midcourse corrections." Life often deals out surprises. And not all surprises are pleasant or welcome.

Surprises can more often than not be very challenging. Sheila gave me a wonderful surprise. I cannot imagine a more wonderful gift than a new little life. That baby turned out to be *another* boy—Scotty—our third.

"Challenging" is a slight understatement when raising a three-year-old, a one-year-old, and a newborn. However, our life was never boring. It was very exciting. It was full of surprises—big and little. We couldn't have done it without relying on each other's support and God's. I thank God every day for the excitement and the vitality that His surprises have brought to our life and to our marriage.

25

Married! A New Name! A New Identity!

"Mrs. James Coleman." I said the words over and over again, trying them on like a new dress. I had to get used to the idea that this was me. A new name, a new role, a new identity—a new me.

I had it all figured out. I was in control. I was going to be the perfect housewife. Our new condominium was going to sparkle like a Pine Sol commercial. I would be sexy, vivacious, and the best cook imaginable. So I donned my apron, got out my polish, my recipe books, my vacuum, and got to work. Unfortunately, I was playing a part in a play. And it wasn't long before I had to leave the stage and deal with reality—real feelings, real emotions, the real me—whoever that was.

I had lived my life at such a frantic pace that I had never looked at myself in the mirror and looked at myself realistically, imperfections and all. I didn't know my strengths or my weaknesses. I didn't know my likes and my dislikes. I didn't know who or what I wanted to be in life. I only knew that I didn't want to be lonely, and if I had to play a role to win the love of the man I loved, then I would play the role. If it meant wearing aprons, if it meant polishing copper-bottomed pans, then I would do it. I longed for, lived for, Jim's love and his approval.

It's always dangerous when you don't know what you really want or you're afraid to tell how you really feel. Since I was not able to be honest with myself or with the one I loved, then it shouldn't have come as too big of a surprise when the act blew up in my face.

My suppressed desires—whatever they were—surfaced angrily, and I lashed out at the one I loved most—Jim.

For instance, when Jim noticed a household task that I had neglected, he mentioned it kindly. "Sheila, when are you going to mop this floor?"

You would have thought Vesuvius was erupting if you had seen and heard my reaction to such a caring "tip." I felt like someone had hit me in the gut. I wasn't doing the job. I wasn't perfect. I was failing at my new role. I didn't deserve Jim's love. It wouldn't be long before he left me for someone far neater and more suited to his needs.

I fled the room and withdrew from him. I wept and wailed. Then I got mad. Who did he think he was anyway? Sure it's easy to spot flaws, but what about all the good things I was doing? Hadn't he seen how my pots shined? Hadn't he seen how hard I was trying to be everything he needed and wanted?

When Jim saw my reaction to his suggestions, he opted for silence. Instead of asking me to vacuum the carpet, he did it himself. That just made me madder. Why is he interfering with my role? The husband of the perfect wife doesn't vacuum! I interpreted his help as yet another slap in the face. I imagined him thinking, *Sheila can't do it herself, so I'll do it for her.* I was convinced that I was not measuring up as a wife.

My identity was so mixed-up, so warped by a pre-conceived image of who and what I should be, that I was unable to be the Sheila that God had lovingly created. It took a long time before I was able to admit to myself and to my husband that I am not a polishing-type of girl—and that's okay.

I am still working at accepting the fact that I am not the housekeeper Jim would like me to be. I still cringe when Jim vacuums. I am tempted to jump up from the computer and take the vacuum out of his hands. I still struggle with feelings of inadequacy when I realize that I'm not everything I think I should be. I do wish that I were better at being a housekeeper. I do wish that I could make my home more sparkly for my artist husband.

However, I know my limitations and have accepted them. I have begun to identify my strengths and talents. I *am* a good writer. I *am* an understanding companion. I *am* fun to be with. I *am* a good cook. I have a strong analytical mind. I *am* creative with words and educational concepts. I *am* a dedicated wife and a terrific mother.

It's exciting to see that many couples today are no longer bound by rigid roles dictated by sex and tradition. Instead they have opted to divide the workload according to strengths and abilities. Men are pitching in. They are helping with the parenting, and most are loving it! It's so exciting to see all these modern fathers changing diapers, cooking, and even cleaning.

It isn't easy for these fathers to break away from the time-honored expectations. They have no role model to show them how to break in and help. And we women don't always make it easy on them. We long for help, but when our husbands give it, we get defensive and territorial. This is my kitchen. Who do you think you are re-organizing my cupboards? Conflicts can easily erupt when identities and self-esteem are based on superficial roles.

I want to be more than an actress, acting out a *role*. I am more interested in being the *real* me, the unique me, the one-of-a-kind me that can't be pushed into a preconceived role. I would hope that we couples will continue to encourage each other in our quest to discover our unique gifts. I would hope that we would acknowledge and support our spouses and ourselves in our quest to develop a strong identity. And as we become acquainted with the real me and the real you that makes up a real relationship, a real marriage, a real friendship, we will be forging bonds that will keep us together—forever.

26

Who's in Control Here, Anyway?

"Blue, Hawaiian moonlight . . ." I sang in my heart, and for good reason. We were on our way to Hawaii— Sheila and I, Jason, age three, Chris, eighteen months, Scotty, six months, and my Aunt Pyhllis, in her late sixties. Altogether, we took up two rows of the airplane. To save on airfare, we decided to each hold a baby for the five-hour flight from LAX to Honolulu. Overflowing diaper bags, sacks of toys, Legos, purses, cameras, coats, blankets—we were a sight.

My wonderful aunt had never married, and she had given many hours to my sister and me when we were small. I wanted to thank her some way for all that she had meant to me. Sheila and I decided to take her to Hawaii. In addition, we felt that three little ones under the age of four were too much to handle alone, even in paradise. Auntie Phyl was delighted to come, but nervous. Airplanes were not her favorite environment.

We got as settled as we could. Auntie Phyl pushed her call button. "I'll take a glass of wine, please." My aunt drinks a glass of wine only on rare occasions. She apparently felt the need to explain her unusual request for she laughed nervously and said, "To calm my nerves. You know how frightened I am of flying, especially over that *immense* ocean!"

Auntie Phyl sat two seats over from me. Little Jason sat between us. Baby Scotty was on my lap. Sheila sat behind me, with strong-willed Christopher on her lap. The stewardess brought Auntie Phyl her glass of wine. I peeked over my shoulder to look at Sheila. Her eyebrows were arched in a surprised look.

The plane was late in taking off—two hours late to be exact. We had used up half of our bag of tricks in the terminal, waiting for take-off. Now the babies were getting restless. The box of Legos fell to the floor. A zillion little red, white, and yellow blocks rolled seemingly throughout the plane. We gathered up what we could—no small feat while balancing an infant on your lap.

Auntie Phyl pushed her call button again. She surreptitiously said to the stewardess, "A refill, please."

I didn't have to sneak a peek at Sheila. I *knew* what she was thinking. I could almost feel her bony finger poking me through my well-padded seat.

Finally, the plane began to move. It taxied, built up speed, and then whoosh—take-off. We were on our way! Hurrah!

Christopher's ears objected. The whole plane knew his ears were plugged. His ear-splitting cries pierced everybody's ears but his own. Sheila tried to plug him up with a bottle. It worked—for a few minutes. He had used up most of it, waiting for the plane to take off. When the sound of air filled the nipple, he resumed his screams of pain and indignation.

Auntie Phyl summoned the stewardess one more time.

Everything seemed to settle down. Christopher settled down and went to sleep. Scotty also took a nap.

Jason looked at a book. I had felt a tingling in one side of my face on take-off, but I didn't think a thing of it until I tried to get a little shut-eye. Then I discovered, to my dismay, that one eye wouldn't close. I tried and tried to push the eyelid closed, but it was as if it was frozen. Auntie Phyl smiled at me. I smiled back. But something felt funny. My aunt said, "Jim, what's the matter with your face?" Only half of my mouth had turned up.

"I don't know," I mumbled. It felt like half of my face was frozen. I couldn't move the tiniest muscle on the entire right side of my face. My right contact lens was drying up. It was my turn to summon the stewardess.

I called her over and explained my problem to her. Just then Sheila woke up to see a crouched stewardess talking to me in hushed, concerned tones. This time she didn't try to be polite. She poked me in no uncertain terms and said, "What's going on, Jim?"

I turned around as best I could, not wanting to awaken sleeping Scotty. I mumbled through half-paralyzed lips, "Half of my face is frozen."

"What?" She looked horrified. "You're joking!"

"No. really."

"Smile," she demanded.

I smiled. Half of my face crinkled into a smile. The other half sat there. "The stewardess is talking to the captain to find out what we should do."

Sheila told me later she feared I was having a stroke. All she could think of was how she was going to manage in Hawaii with three babies, an aunt, and a husband with a stroke.

The stewardess returned, "The captain says we can turn around and go back if you want to," she said.

Turn back?! Who're they kidding?! After waiting two hours to take off? I thought. *We were two and a half hours into the flight at this point. The L1011 is jammed. I'll take my chances with a stroke. Who knows what three hundred angry, disappointed people, who'd already had to endure Christopher's cries would do?* These thoughts all flashed through my mind. The choice was clear. "I feel okay to go on," I mumbled.

"Well, if you're sure." The stewardess relayed the message to the captain. I felt as comfortable as I could with my decision. Sheila kept poking me. "Are you okay?"

I tried to downplay the situation. I didn't like the looks I was starting to get from the other passengers. The stewardess came by again and said, "The captain said to try this. It's a long shot, but sometimes it helps with this kind of freakish incident."

I cringed at her use of the word "freak," but took the smelling salts she held out. She broke the small packet, and I took a deep breath of the fumes. The gas penetrated the cavities in my head and apparently released trapped pressure. I turned to look at Sheila and smiled—with my whole face! "It worked!"

"Thank Heaven!" she exclaimed.

The rest of the trip went smoothly enough. But for some reason the stewardess gave us a wide berth. I can't say I blame her.

This little incident was a lesson to me. I like to be in control. I always assumed that I would be in control in my marriage as a husband and as a father. I thought that my wife would always do what I expected her to do, mostly because she loved me, but also because I was the head of the family. I foolishly believed that I could ask or tell my children to do something, and they would do it. Of course, it wasn't long before I realized that I could repeat instructions, requests, demands—over and over and over—only to be ignored—over and over and over. I can't tell you how frustrating this has been for me.

I know I am not alone in my frustrations. I have heard my male colleagues and friends express these same feelings. Overall, men seem to suffer from hero syndrome. We feel that we have to be in charge. We have to be in control of the situation, because ultimately we feel responsible. Society told us we should be responsible. Our fathers provided a model of responsibility.

But then we ran smack dab into life. We found ourselves in marriages with children and financial situations that felt overwhelming. Our lives flew out of control. We found ourselves flying over the ocean with our family, literally or figuratively—our full responsibility. And often we discover, as in my case, that we not only don't have control of the whole situation, we don't even have control of our own bodies.

Those times are a fact of life. And I believe God allows them because they force us to face the fact that we need help. We need to ask someone else to share the load. We need to relax and let the captain of the plane take over the controls.

I'm *slowly* coming around. I'm learning that my children are not marionettes. Thank God! I am learning that we are all individuals made in His image. Each of us is a unique and miraculous creation, not made to be fully controlled by anybody but God.

When I let go of the controls and allow Jesus to pilot my life, I find that my burdens grow lighter. And quite honestly that's when the wonderful extemporaneous things happen in the lives of my children and family that really make life a joy.

I'm still reluctant to let go, but I know that God has made me aware of my need to let go. As long as I respond positively to His nudging, we'll all be going places— together.

135

27

Response-Ability

The pain was worse than I expected! I felt like I was going to die. I screamed at the nurse, "Take it! Take it! Call the doctor and tell him I want a Caesarean. I'm not going to go through one more of those . . . uhggg!!"

"Now, now, Mrs. Coleman. It won't be much longer. I'm sure that you'll have this baby before the day's over." If I'd had a dart I would have thrown it at her. I was beginning to understand why they took away all my personal belongings when I checked into this house of horrors.

And where was Jim? Fine for him to be able to go to the dining room anytime he got hungry. What did he think this was—a retreat? I felt like I was dying, I *needed* him, and he says, real calmlike, "I'm hungry. I'm going to go get a bite of dinner before they close the cafeteria." He had used the same line for breakfast and lunch, and now it was dinner time. Nobody ever said it would take so *long!*

"Ugghhh!" that pain was strong. Where was Jim? He was supposed to be coaching me through these contractions! I called the nurse. "I'm sure that this baby's ready to be born. That was a . . . Uggghhh!" She looked at the monitor. "Yes! That's more like it. You're making progress now. Oh, wow! There goes your water!"

No kidding! I expected some moisture, not gallons all over the bed. Suddenly the urge to bear down took over. I felt as though I were going to burst. The nurse suddenly transformed into a drill sergeant. She stuck her nose in my face and hollered at me. "Pant! Pant! Pant! Pant! Don't talk! Pant!"

I panted. And hyperventilated. She stuck an oxygen mask on my face. Just then Jim walked into the labor room, bearing his tray of hospital cuisine, complete with jiggling, green Jell-O. I was going fast. The nurse was hollering at me with every contraction. The doctor came in and declared that I could push. They hustled me into the delivery room, oxygen mask and all, leaving Jim behind with his green Jell-O. He dropped his plate and raced to catch up.

Fifteen minutes later our first son was born. We laughed. We hugged. We cried. We couldn't believe we had done such a great thing together. Jim and I took complete credit for this absolutely, beautiful, perfect little boy.

We reveled in our brief glimpse of heaven. We drank in his tender beauty, marveled at our little angel for the first four days. Then he suddenly emerged from the trauma of birth, no longer content to sleep through the day and the night, and woke up hungry and crying. I'd feed him, but he would still cry. Where was the nurse now that I needed her? I was on my own.

It took some doing, but I began to interpret Jason's cries. Based on what I knew about him, I could tell if he needed more food, his diaper changed, or just some sleep. I began to be sensitive to his needs and to respond accordingly.

Jim and I loved this little baby. We were both surprised by the intensity of our feelings for our son. But to be honest, I was also afraid. There were times when this helpless little baby was curled up on my bosom, when I was overwhelmed with the idea of the responsibility I had accepted when I had chosen to be a mother. (I have since discovered that thoughts such as these are common.) I felt responsible for his happiness, his health, his future, his well-being. The person that he would become would be a direct result of the care I had given him.

Those thoughts began to weigh heavily on me. I felt paralyzed by the overwhelming sense of responsibility. One day I called Jim at work. "Jim, I'm so afraid that I'm doing it all wrong. What if I say or do something that emotionally scars Jason for the rest for his life? What if I don't watch him carefully enough? What if I'm not feeding him the right kind of foods? What if . . ."

Jim stopped me from my barrage of what ifs. He said, "Sheila, don't worry about it. You're not in this alone, you know. He's my son, too. God wouldn't have given him to us if He didn't think we could handle it."

"Okay. Yeah, you're right. I'm sorry I got so caught up in my fears."

A few days later, I read my Bible while Jason slept. I prayed and this thought came to me. I believe it was God speaking to me and saying, "Look closely at the word *responsibility*." Suddenly I read it the way God wanted me to read it, as two separate words, *response ability.*

I realized that my responsibility in relationships is not to control, not to mold, not to change, not to make over, but to *respond* to the best of my *ability* to my loved ones' needs. Nothing more. Nothing less.

My responsibility as a mother is to respond to my children's needs. When they are discouraged, I respond with encouragement. When they need love, I wrap my arms around them. When they need discipline, I ask them to take responsibility for their own behavior. Of course, sometimes my responses to their needs have been negative or inappropriate. Usually, those have been times when I have taken on more responsibility than God intended me to have.

My responsibility as a wife is similar to my responsibilities as a mother. I simply need to respond to Jim's needs. Does he need a friend today? A listening ear? Time and privacy to work it out alone? Does he need a concrete expression of love from me—like a freshly starched shirt, or fresh towels, or a note tucked into his briefcase? It's not easy being alert to Jim's needs and being able to decipher them. It takes patience and consideration. I can't pry it out of him. But I can be there when he is ready to talk.

It's not my responsibility as a wife or as a mother to fix my loved ones' problems, to manage their lives, or control their behavior. After all, how arrogant it is to think that I have so much to offer. Quite the contrary, God has simply called me to *respond* to my loved ones' needs to the best of my *ability*—and leave the results to Him. It is a liberating way to live and to love—for all concerned!

28

And Seldom Is Heard a Discouraging Word

I needed a change. I knew it in my heart. But I couldn't admit to myself that I needed to move on. I was too afraid to step out of my comfort zone to even toy with the idea.

I had been working for my parents at the Crystal Cathedral Ministries for nearly twenty years. My office was right next door to my husband's. My mother's office was down the hall. Dad's was in the next building. My sister was new on staff, as was my brother-in-law. It was truly a family affair, and it was all that I had experienced in the way of work.

My job had been challenging and fulfilling at the beginning, but as my children came and grew and started their schooling, I found myself drawn more and more into their classroom as a volunteer aide. I gave one day a week to the classroom, and I got hooked by the little faces, the never-ending surprises, the questions, the needs of these little lives. When I returned to the office, I found that all I wanted to do was to talk about what I had experienced the previous day in the classroom. I couldn't get those children out of my mind.

Although my responsibilities at the offices of the Crystal Cathedral were creative, and included planning the famous inspirational televised Sunday morning programs, I was not finding the fulfillment that I longed for. I felt like I was missing something that God wanted me to do with my life. The job had become just a job. I began to feel a hint that I was supposed to work with children.

My dissatisfaction at the office grew. I became moody. I fought depression. I questioned my value as a contributor to the Kingdom of God. Jim watched and waited until I was ready to ask for his help.

His patience was rewarded one day at lunch. I sat opposite him and grumbled, "I feel guilty working here. My heart's not in this anymore. I don't feel right taking money to do a half-hearted job."

Jim smiled lovingly. "We all go through times when we're not as enthusiastic as we should be. I wonder if there's something else that's bothering you."

I nodded. It was hard to put it into words, to admit that my job with my family, with the church that had been a major part of my entire life, was no longer what I wanted to devote myself to. I said. "I'm not fulfilled working for the ministry any more." There, I said it.

"I can tell you're not as happy there as you used to be," he said.

"No, I'm not. I've gotten to the point where I have lost all faith in my abilities. I don't know if I have anything to contribute or not. I need to find out if I have gifts, talents, abilities apart from my family. My identity has been wrapped up in this ministry for so long that I need to reclaim Sheila. I need to get reacquainted with her and get to know her strengths and abilities."

"What would you do if you weren't working at the church?" he asked.

Without hesitation I exclaimed, "I'd be a teacher!"

"You would?"

The idea came as much as a surprise to me as it did to Jim. "What would it take to be a teacher?"

"I suppose I'd have to go back to school. I really don't know what it would take." (I have my B.A., but I haven't taken early education courses.)

Jim looked at me and said, "Why don't you call around and ask some questions?"

So, I called—one year later. It took that long to get up the nerve. And when I did call, I was disappointed. The local university offered only a full-time program. That program was out of the question, especially in light of the fact that I still had a toddler at home. I discarded the idea and decided to stick with volunteering as a parent aide.

A few months later Jim cornered me at lunch again. "I haven't heard you say anything about your idea to be a teacher. Are you still thinking about it or have you dropped the idea altogether?"

I cringed. I didn't want to be reminded about it. I had been so put off by the brusque, inflexible attitude of our local university that I had tried to bury the dream. As if he could read my mind Jim said, "I know you were disappointed when you inquired into the teacher education program, but haven't you called any other places? It's not like you to give up so easily, Sheila."

"So easily!? The thought of going back to school, working part time, and keeping a home going with four boys feels overwhelming!" I snapped.

"Yes. I can see where it would. What would happen if you quit work and went back to school?"

Hmmm. Here was a schedule that could work. "Don't we need the money I bring in?"

"We can manage without it. We'll have to readjust our priorities . . . but I know we can do it if we *want* to."

"Really?"

"Really."

Encouraged, I called another local college. I found, to my delight that they had a program tailor-made to my schedule. It was a part-time program, with evening and Saturday classes. And the program dovetailed with the master's program, so I could get my master's in education while working toward my credentials. The people were so pleasant and accommodating, that I called Jim excitedly. "I'm going to do it! I'm going to quit my job and go back to school."

"I'm glad! You have a lot to offer children," he said.

"Do you really think so?"

"Without a doubt."

It wasn't easy leaving a ministry that I loved. Telling my parents that I was quitting was one of the hardest things I've ever had to do. I felt like a traitor, like I was turning my back on them. Yet, in my heart of hearts, I knew that God was calling me to do something new with my life. And it felt good to have a dream all of my own, on my own.

It took a great deal of courage to go back to college. When I told my four boys about my decision, Jason, our ten-year-old said, "Oh, Mom! This is soooo embarrassing!"

"Why?" I asked, taken aback.

"Does this mean we'll sit at football games and watch you jump and cheer with those guys throwing you in the air?" (It seems his only impression so far of college life is the cheerleaders with the short skirts we've seen at college football games.) I laughed. "No. You won't have to worry about that!"

I thought I had retained some of my youthful appearance, until I stepped on campus with eighteen- and nineteen-year-old girls. (I knew immediately I'd never make the pep squad!) Would my mind still be able to retain information? Would I still be able to learn? Could I pass the tests required to get my credentials?

There were many nervous days, mornings when I rose at dawn to take a standardized test, afternoons when I met with my adviser, evenings when I went to my first class. My life was suddenly filled with butterflies. But every step of the way Jim encouraged me:

- "You can do it."
- "I'll help you find the time to study."
- "We'll go out for a hamburger on the nights you have class, so you won't have to come home to dishes."
- "You don't need to worry. You know a lot about children."
- "I knew you'd do well on your test."

I can't tell you how good it feels to be following my heart's call. It hasn't been easy. There are nights when I burn the midnight lamp, trying to get an assignment completed on time. Some papers I find so exciting they nearly consume me. I get so caught up in what I'm learning that I become oblivious to the ones around me whom I love. But I'm learning. I'm readjusting. I'm growing. And Jim's support has enabled me, freed me, encouraged me to become all that I can be. What a precious gift he has given me.

Part 4

Give It Time

Being Friends for Life Means Giving a Priority to Our Relationship with Each Other and with God

Dear Lord,

You have set our world in motion. You have hurled the planets in their courses. You have ordained that life should have a beginning and an end. You have created sunrises and sunsets, seasons of life, cycles of living and loving. You have created us—alone and together—in Your image as creatures of choice.

The sands in the hourglass are swiftly slipping by. Give us the wisdom to use wisely the time You have given us:

Time for weeping
        and time for laughing,
Time for being alone
        and time for being together,
Time for forgiving
        and time for accepting forgiveness,
Time for playing
        and time for praying.

Help us keep our priorities in the proper order so that we may take the time to glory in Your creation. Give us the strength to give up that which is unimportant and to give to You and to each other our very best. Help us make our choices so that we may not regret precious moments wasted and daily we may glorify You.

Amen.

To everything there is a season,
A time for every purpose under heaven.

Ecclesiastes 3:1

29

Date Night

I was petrified! I had heard about all the horrible things that happened to "pea-greeners" (this was the name attached to the first-year junior high school students in 1962). Yes, my first day and week in the seventh grade were humbling.

The Friday afternoon of that first week, my new English teacher (English was my final period of the day) asked the class to write a brief paper on "Your Favorite Part of Your First Week in Junior High School."

The content of my paper was never in question. "I'm glad that it's Friday!" I wrote, "and the wonderful weekend is ahead!"

It was probably not exactly what she had in mind. I don't remember my grade on that particular paper. But I'll never forget the warm fuzzy feelings I got thinking about Friday night at my home with my family.

Friday night was popcorn night. It always had been as long as I could remember. Popcorn! How I loved that fragrant, buttery snack. And nice tall ice-laced grape soda, all my own to enjoy. The Flintstones were new on television about that time. Popcorn, soda, and the Flintstones, along with my family, in the warmth of our home. Who could ask for more?

My soul lived for this precious window of time each Friday. Not that I thought of or did anything else. My life was full of adventures, bike rides, fun, chores, schoolwork. But Friday represented to me peace, contentment, no pressures, warmth, fellowship, acceptance.

I'm thankful for my childhood family and memories like this that have become the substance of a healthy adult. As I grew into senior high school, college, employment, the complexion of my Friday nights changed. But that childhood "warm fuzzy" of letting go of everything else for a time of relaxation on Friday night remained. And it remained that way up to the time I met, dated, and married Sheila. It's still with me.

When I fell in love with Sheila, she became the highlight of my life. It was only natural that my Friday nights began to include her. How I looked forward to her company in a loose, unstructured, pressure-free environment. Apparently she felt or developed the same feelings about it. I do not ever recall discussing it or making a pat rule, "Friday night is our date night." But that's what happened.

Every Friday night of our married life has been spent with each other. Alone. No double dates. No company. No children. No meetings. No nothing! Just me and Sheila, husband and wife. The babysitter shows up at 6 P.M., and we're out the door. It's a time we relish, cherish, and guard *selfishly*. It's okay to be selfish, hard-headed, and stubborn to protect a principle that is so critical it must remain immovable.

There have been exceptions. On our date night we have gone together, once or twice, to visit a friend or relative's new baby, or to visit a sick friend. But the exceptions to our rule of complete seclusion are few and far, far apart. In twelve years, Sheila and I have gone out on our date night more than six hundred times! Probably only on ten or twelve of those nights did we spend a brief amount of our precious time in visits to new mothers and babies, or sick relatives and friends.

The Bible tells me that God rested on the seventh day. He commanded us to do likewise, "Remember the Sabbath day, to keep it holy." I like to think that our date night is part of our weekly sabbath. One day in seven, we enjoy each other in a pressure-free environment. We give our marriage a chance to refresh, renew, to rest.

What do we do on our date night? For our first five years of marriage we went to the same restaurant and usually sat in the same booth. For five years straight! Once a week, every Friday night, same restaurant, same booth, same time.

Boring? Hardly. When you've both been swamped all week, a dinner alone together is the most wonderful therapy imaginable. We enjoy one another's company. It's all the more rich over a relaxing cup of coffee. Most of the time we talk. Sometimes we don't. We have developed a sense that each of us needs a little time to leave behind the pressures of the day and/or the week. Sometimes it's hard and uncomfortable. One of us will drag the emotions of a frustrating day or situation into the sanctified pasture of our date night. Then, we're there for each other to work out the remaining pressures (just like a good back rub), to talk about it, and to encourage the other to leave it behind.

Sometimes our Friday night dinner can last two or three hours!

After dinner we walk around. We talk some more. Sometimes we walk around and "shop" in our favorite mall. We love to look at the beautiful things, and it doesn't have to cost a dime if we don't buy anything. Other times we walk along the boardwalk at our favorite beach.

Most of the time we center our date night on each other. Face to face. Talk and more talk. Most of the time we need this interaction with each other. But every fifth or sixth date night we go to a movie. There we laugh together. We try to see happy, funny, redeeming movies. We want our lives to be happy, funny, and redeeming. Violence, horror, and explicit, immoral sexual scenes have no place in our lives. We are what we read or see, and we choose to bring positive values and memories into our hearts and our home.

Date night has become a bond for Sheila and me. We both look forward to it like *nothing else we do each week.*

I believe in the commitment I verbalized on my wedding day. To maintain our marriage relationship, we have found our weekly date night rendezvous to be the single most important act we do together as man and wife.

My father-in-law puts it this way (sorry this isn't very romantic, but guys understand this kind of talk), "I wouldn't think of buying and running a new car without regularly scheduled maintenance. Oil and lube at six thousand miles. (Don't forget to rotate the tires, too.) Change lugs and points at fifteen thousand miles." My marriage to my dear wife is not totally unlike this. Our relationship requires regularly scheduled maintenance.

It's true. Our marriages are holy in God's eyes. He asks and expects us to give them careful attention to detail. We can't have lives together without spending time together.

30

Repaired for Christmas

All four boys were tucked in bed. The glow of the lights seeped through the shutters and bounced off the walls of their darkened rooms. Faint echoes of carols drifted up the stairs to lull them asleep. The scene was so idyllic, so contrary to what awaited me throughout the rest of the house, that I longed to linger in the peaceful rooms, to curl up next to one of my sons and rest my worn-out old bones. But there was so much left to do before I could call it a day.

Little children would undo Christmas as fast as I could do it. Normally I wouldn't let these setbacks bother me. But this year they did. I was feeling pressured. I had agreed to lead a Bible study for the women at the Crystal Cathedral. They had given me a topic: How does a mother of four boys prepare for Christmas?

The subject gnawed at me as I worked to prepare my house for Christmas. I am not the visually artistic one in the family. I don't know where to begin when it comes to decorating, and I am usually disappointed with my attempts, especially at Christmastime.

I linger every year at the checkout stand of the grocery store, awestruck by the glorious pictures of gingerbread houses resplendent in confectionary details. How do they do it? How do they make these masterpieces? I had read several of the instructions, but I had never dared to attempt such an overwhelming undertaking.

But this year I was determined to create an entire gingerbread village. Even the boys helped. They made their houses out of graham crackers. My confidence soared. I got lost in my own creation and built a charming clock tower. I used a sugar cone for the tower and decorated the entire cone with silver sugar beads. It gleamed and glistened and looked every bit as wonderful as I had imagined. My artistic ten-year-old said, "Wow, Mom! That looks great!"

Of course, the kitchen was a disaster. There were trails of powdered sugar footprints on the floor. Every inch of counter space was covered with mixing bowls, spoons, and bags of assorted candies and cookies. I was glad Jim wasn't home. But the mess could be cleaned up. What mattered was that we had *prepared* for Christmas.

I looked for the right spot to display our village and found a piece of glittered "snow" to spread on the bottom of the window sill.

Then I picked up my masterpiece—my clock tower. As I was setting it in place, the top of the tower nicked the bottom of the cupboard. That tiny nudge shattered the entire clock. Silver beads fell and rolled all over the kitchen. I had finally created something beautiful, only to destroy it!

Suddenly I felt overwhelmed by Christmas preparations. I was spending more time fixing things than I was creating. My list was growing longer instead of shorter.

I sat dejectedly at the kitchen table. The bowls needed to be washed. The floor needed to be scrubbed. The couch needed to be cleaned.

Where should I start? I looked at the shattered mess that had been my clock tower. Suddenly I remembered there was a sugar cone left over. Maybe it wouldn't be too much work to redo it. It would only require one more batch of frosting.

My resolve to remake the clock tower gave me new confidence. I thought of the rest of the house and decided that I could repair most of the damage fairly easily.

Then panic set in again. *Tomorrow's the day I talk to the women. What am I going to say?* I wondered. How does a mother of four prepare for Christmas? Suddenly it hit me. A mother of four doesn't *prepare* for Christmas. A mother of four *repairs* for Christmas. Of course! I could talk for hours on that theme! I'm an expert at repairing! And after all, isn't that the message of Christmas? Didn't Christ come to repair our mistakes?

No one's perfect. I learn every day how I could have done it better. A book, a teacher, or a child shows me how much I still have to learn. And when I begin to berate myself for making a mistake, Jesus reminds me that I care. Jesus reminds me that I am learning. He gives me the courage to say, "I'm sorry." And He encourages me with a hug or a note from a boy that says, "I love you. You're the best Mom in the world."

And just when I'm feeling lonely in my marriage, just when I get distracted and neglect my husband's needs, Jesus nudges me and pushes me out into Jim's world. He draws me into the garage to talk to my biggest boy as he works on his boy toys, his cars and his engines. He gives me simple ideas, like putting on a pot of coffee and inviting Jim in to have a cup.

In my marriage, Jesus repairs my most common mistake of neglecting my husband, my friend for life. He reminds me of my priorities. He renews my ability to give to my husband. He forgives me and teaches me to for- give myself. He encourages me to keep on, to persevere, to give myself and my marriage time.

I'll never be fully prepared for Christmas or for marriage or for parenting. But repaired? With Christ's help—you bet!

31

Even Grandmas Make Mistakes

Date night is the highlight of our week! It is Sheila's job to find the babysitter, and it's not always easy. We are more fortunate than most in that we have so much family nearby. Grandpas and Grandmas pitch in on a regular basis.

It's no easy task babysitting four boys. They are a rambunctious handful. Between bottles, diapers, wrestling matches, you name it, babysitting our boys is challenging to say the least. My in-laws have an extremely demanding schedule. Nevertheless, they manage to work in some nights when they can babysit. I can't tell you how much it means to the boys to have their grandparents over. Date night is as much a highlight for them as it is for us!

One date night Sheila and I were rushing out the door as always. Our hours alone are precious and we are eager to beat the traffic and the waiting lines at the restaurants. Sheila raced through the last-minute instructions for her mother, pointing out the bedtime bottle in the fridge, the ice cream, date night treat for the older boys, emergency phone numbers, medicine for Nicky's bronchitis, and extra diapers as she grabbed her coat and purse. We kissed our boys, one, two, three, four, "Good night! See you in the morning!"

Unbeknownst to us, while we were savoring our seclusion, complete pandemonium broke out at home. My father-in-law is pretty helpless as a babysitter. He's a terrific preacher, but he's much less effective when it comes to child care. Even though he comes along to help, my mother-in-law carries the bulk of the burden.

However, Sheila and I didn't give a thought to any problems at home. Her parents had successfully raised five children. What were four little boys? Nicky could be a handful, because he was still a baby, but we felt confident that Mom could manage. After a tranquil dinner, we decided to see a movie. There was no hurry to get home. It was late when we finally arrived back home. We came through the back door and found her mother and father asleep on the couch. They looked pretty well done in.

"Mom? Dad? We're home," we said.

They sat up and looked pretty bleary-eyed. "Oh! I'm sorry. We fell asleep."

"Are you okay?" we asked.

"Sure." They didn't look okay.

Dad looked at Mom and said nervously, "Well, are you going to tell them or shall I?"

"Tell us what?" Sheila inquired.

Her mother shuffled her feet and said, "I suppose I have to tell you. The boys will spill the beans in the morning, anyway, and I'd rather it came from me than from them."

"Mom!" Sheila pressed. "What is it? Tell me what happened here tonight."

"Well, you know you asked me to give Nicky his medicine?"

"Yes," she responded apprehensively.

"Well, I gave him the teaspoonful as you told me to. Nicky really fought it. He pulled a terrible face and fussed a lot, but I held him down and forced it into his mouth. He tried to spit it out, but I held his lips shut."

"Really? He doesn't usually mind taking his medicine. The pharmacist puts so much sugar in it that he thinks it's candy."

"Well, I don't think the pharmacist put sugar in *this* bottle of medicine. You see, I gave him the wrong medicine."

"What do you mean?" Sheila and I were getting nervous.

"After he took it, I looked at the bottle to make sure that I had remembered the correct dosage."

My father-in-law picked up the story for her. He said, "Suddenly, I heard her scream. She didn't yell. She *screamed!* Like she'd been stabbed! She was crying, 'Oh No! Oh No! The medicine I gave Nicky was for Autumn!' "

Autumn is our anorectic Irish Setter. She's the skinniest dog you'd ever hope to see. She can't help it. We can't help it. We feed her, but it looks like she's starving to death. It's really embarrassing. In fact one day I found a bag of dog food that somebody had thrown over the fence. The vet says she's okay, but he gave us some medicine for her to fatten her up.

I couldn't believe Sheila's mother had given our baby the dog's medicine! (Good help is getting harder and harder to find.)

"You gave Nicky Autumn's medicine!?" Sheila exclaimed.

"Oh, I felt terrible!" Mom said.

"She really did," Dad concurred.

"I called the poison control center right away," she added.

"You did?" I smiled at the thought of what the poison control center would say about *this!* Sheila asked, "What did they say?"

"They put me on hold."

"I'll bet."

"They said they never had this problem happen before."

"Probably not."

"They checked their computers, but they couldn't find that medicine in their records."

"Mmmm. They probably don't get too many calls for babies poisoned by dog medicine," I reasoned.

"No. That's what they said. They suggested calling the vet and asking him what the prescription was for."

"And did you do that?" I asked.

"Yes. I think we got him out of bed. He sounded pretty sleepy. Anyway, he said not to worry. It was just a strong concentrate of vitamins. It was just to help fatten her up, he said. It shouldn't hurt anyone."

We couldn't keep a straight face any longer. Sheila and I laughed and said, "It sounds like you had quite a night."

"Oh. We did! I hope Nicky's okay."

"I'm sure he's fine," Sheila said, trying to reassure her.

"I'm really sorry."

"Don't worry about it. Thank you for helping out."

The boys excitedly shared the story with us first thing the next morning. "You should have heard Grandma scream!" Jason said. "I didn't know she could get so excited!"

"She gave Nicky dog medicine," Chris added. "No wonder Nicky tried to spit it out."

"Nicky's no dummy."

Just then the phone rang. Sheila answered. It was her mother. "Sheila, I had to call. I have really been worried about Nicky. Is he okay?"

Seizing the moment, Sheila replied, "Well, I checked him over this morning. His hair is pretty shiny. His nose is wet. And he's been barking orders at me."

"Oh!" she laughed. "That's mean!" she said.

"No, really, he's fine. Don't worry. It's one of the funniest stories I've ever heard!"

She sounded relieved but added, "I can't believe I did such a stupid thing."

"It's not easy keeping your wits about you when you've got these four creative boys to take care of," Sheila said.

"Well, it can get really confusing," she agreed.

"Very."

Mistakes. Even Grandmas and Grandpas make them. And getting along with in-laws isn't always easy, but it can be pretty exciting and even funny when you mesh two different families together. The connections we feel when we laugh and play with our spouses and with our extended families are only possible if we are willing to give it time. It takes time to get to know each other and time to grow closer together. I have never regretted the time I have invested in my family, but, then, they are a pretty lively bunch.

32

Make a Memory

Jim loves to sail. Don't ask me why. The boat has barely left the dock and he frequently finds himself leaning over the side, heaving up his supper. Yet that never stops him. It would me! I can't stand discomfort. Give me a roaring fire and a good book to read any day.

When you consider how sick Jim gets when he sails, and when you know how much I crave comfort, it is a minor miracle that Jim and I spent as much time sailing as we did when we first got married. Jim claims to this day that sailing and boats lure him in a mysterious way. He loves the salty air, the tang of the sea, the sails snapping in the wind, the slap of the waves against the hull.

Often early in our marriage, we would race down to the beach on our date night and try to get a sail in before it got too dark. We rented a tiny little sailboat that we took out into Newport Harbor. I went along because I was still an insecure newlywed and not ready to rock the relationship with too much honesty.

It takes a first-class sailor, like Jim, to get a sailboat through the harbor. There was rarely enough of a breeze in that sheltered waterway to get very far, very fast. Most days we inched through the bay and muttered the sailor's prayer, "Give us this day our daily breeze." Just a whisper would get us home. Just a ripple was all we needed to get back for a long awaited cup of coffee.

Jim took me sailing several times in our first year of marriage. And when Jim told me happily that he had reserved our little boat for the last sail of the season, I said bravely, "Fine. Provided it will be an easy sail." I added as I rubbed my eight-month belly, "Go easy on the tacks and I'll agree to come. It's hard enough diving through those sheets [sheets are ropes tied to the ends of the sails—but sailors *never* call them anything but 'sheets'!] when I'm in good condition. I don't relish the thought of being thrown into premature labor."

It was a cold, blustery evening. We had the wind we always longed for. The boat skimmed through the harbor at record speed. We fairly flew past docks, moorings, and fishermen pulling in the catch of the day. The sun dipped quickly. And once it was gone, the air turned frigid. Chills ran through my bones. I had to admit through my shivering teeth that the view was glorious. There isn't a sight that can compare with the sun setting in beautiful Newport Harbor, the ripples reflecting the day's final rays, the rows of masts, the glorious fire-streaked sky.

The exhilarating ride, while our attention was focused on the glorious view, had carried us farther away from our port than we had wished. We now discovered that we had sailed farther out than ever before. It was late and getting dark—fast.

Jim whipped the little boat around and began his series of tacks into the wind. He cut the prow of the boat as close as he could into the biting wind. We heeled at treacherous angles, taking on water from time to time. At one point we would be riding high, the sail cutting through the frigid wind. Then, suddenly, Jim would holler, "Prepare to come about!" Those words were my cue to dive through the sheets to pull the sail around and tighten the sail as Jim artfully guided the rudder.

This was never an easy part of sailing for me and my long legs. When the tacks were especially sharp I would come face to face with a wall of sea mist as I dove across the boat. It always made me nervous, and I always marveled at how we could come so close to capsizing. How agile we needed to be to keep our footing, our balance, all the while avoiding the boom and sheets lunging from side to side.

That night, the tacks were especially rough, partly because of the strong winds, and partly because Jim was in such a hurry to get back. It was dark. Cold. We had taken on water. I was wet, not to mention tired. How many times had I hurled my out-of-balance body from side to side? How many times had I lunged across this craft? How many more times could I stand to hear those infamous words, "Prepare to come about"?

Yet somehow I lived through it. My legs were wobbly when we got to shore. I was shivering, hungry, and weary. I couldn't wait to get into the warm restaurant and wrap my hands around a hot cup of coffee. Warm, buttered bread and a hot steak sounded like heaven. It was! Although it was nearly ten o'clock before we got to dinner, as I recall that was one of the best meals I ever ate. It was without doubt the best cup of coffee I ever had.

Sailing when you're pregnant on a blustery night is not my idea of fun! Yet I will never forget it. It stands out amongst my most memorable moments. Strangely enough there are times when I find myself longing for the exhilaration of that night.

Those early days of marriage, when we did anything to please our spouse, when we conquered mountains, sailed high seas, those days of adventure were frequently tough, challenging, even painful, but oh how exciting they were! How rewarding! How exhilarating! What have I lost in my quest for comfort?

Complacency? Boredom? Has the relationship grown stale? If we don't talk, soon there's nothing left to talk about. If we let the television provide all of the excitement, there's nothing to be excited about together. In the process we miss out on life—and love.

My father always points out that "a rut is nothing more than a grave with the ends knocked out." We all need surprises, moments of spontaneity, small—adventures . . . these memories are ours alone . . . and, in all likelihood, our most exciting ones!

Ruts. They're so easy to get into. They're comfortable. Safe. You know what to expect. So what's wrong with them? Why do people complain about being in a rut? Perhaps, it's because they are so predictable. There is little excitement in safety, after all. So, what do we want? Excitement or safety? Predictable routine or risky adventure? Comfort or exhilaration? The truth is that we all need and crave a little of both. And we can't really appreciate the one without the other.

Not all the time we spend together making memories can be as exhilarating as the memorable sail. Sometimes we make memories by being in the quiet safety of just sitting, holding hands in comfortable silence. When we take the time to make memories together that will last a lifetime, we are cementing a love that binds us together.

33

Play, Pray, Pay

The words are as clear to me today as they were seventeen years ago, the first time I read them. It was 1975. I did not know Jesus as my personal Lord and Savior—yet. However, my interest in spiritual matters had been piqued as a result of working for the Hour of Power television ministry as their art director.

As a graphic artist I prepared all the artwork for all their printed pieces. Consequently, a lot of words and phrases came across my art table everyday.

"Play, Pray, Pay" caught my eyes. I had noticed that this Schuller guy always rhymed words to catch the reader's attention and make them easy to read and remember. Even I recognized the sale-ability of ideas structured like this.

"Play, Pray, Pay." I looked closer and began to read with mild interest. The article read,

If you want to live an enthusiastic Christian life you should consider these three things:

1. *Play.* Who are your friends? Whom do you fellowship with? Are they a positive or negative influence on you?

2. *Pray.* Talk to God . . . and listen. Seek His guidance.
3. *Pay.* God asks for 10 percent of your income to do His work.

I stopped reading. I thought, *Play, okay, I could brush up on my relationships. Pray, I can pray.* (In fact, I had already started to pray, and it was making a difference. God had begun to work in my heart, even though I had not yet asked Him in.) *Pay? No Way!*

I had my budget all figured. There was definitely no room to give 10 percent to any church. And besides, I reasoned, God doesn't really need money. He owns the cattle on a thousand hills. I'll keep my money.

When you pray, God really works dramatic changes. So I wasn't surprised, only a few weeks later, when I found myself writing out a check for precisely 10 percent of my income and putting it into a small church envelope to place in the offering plate. It seemed like the most natural thing in the world. Much to my amazement, in a very short time I was discovering that when you "Play, Pray, and Pay" God takes care of the rest.

Since that time I have never questioned or doubted my tithing. It's not a bill that we pay every month. It's a pledge to God to return to Him a small portion of His abundance on our lives.

When Sheila and I wed, we never wavered from it. We have always given at least 10 percent of our gross income. Tithing, like prayer, was important to Sheila as it was to me. Her value system reflected her upbringing. Naturally, she had heard about play, pray, and pay all her life.

Consequently, we made the commitment to tithe consistently. And we have never regretted that decision. Time and again we have seen the results of a good and loving God at work in our lives. We thank Him for His goodness by contributing to His church so that it can reach out to other hearts.

When Sheila stopped working recently to go back to school for her master's in education, we agreed that we would continue to give God the same offering. We wouldn't cut back on the tithe, even though our income was significantly lower.

We felt the pinch immediately. "Jim, the kids need new pants."

"Can't it wait a couple of weeks? Until payday?"

"Sure," she'd say reluctantly.

I'd given her the same answer last month when she'd asked me the same question.

"I need to go shopping for groceries, Jim."

"Already?" I'd say. "It seems like you just went."

These lines sounded familiar too.

"My tooth hurts again, Mom," I overheard seven-year-old Scotty say to his mother.

Sheila looked at me. Her eyes hurt. I hurt too.

She said gently, "Scotty's had a cavity for a while now. I've been afraid to ask you if we can take him to the dentist."

At that moment I knew that something had to give. I remembered my mother sitting on the floor when I was a child, bills all around her. While she wiped a tear, she cried, "Where will it all come from?"

Now here I was, nearly thirty years later, with a family of my own, asking the same question. Scotty's tooth was clearly the catalyst. Quite simply, the car, the house, the water, the electricity, the gas, the insurance, the exterminator, and other odds and ends had taken so much that nothing was left for everyday happenings or a minor emergency, like a cavity.

What could we do? Sheila and I developed a plan together. We juggled the mortgage, adjusting the principle. We sold a relatively new car and paid cash for an older one. That relieved us of a *big* monthly payment.

One other area needed attention. Sheila and I discussed our tithe. We prayed about it. Then discussed it again. We prayerfully concluded that we would cut it back to reflect a true 10 percent of my income, no longer including the additional portion we at first elected not to cut out after Sheila's decision to stop working and go back to school.

Because our conclusion was reached by prayer we felt no guilt. I do not believe that God asks us to feel guilty. He wants us to feel redeemed. He gave His Son as final payment to set us *free!*

I honestly, prayerfully, feel that our children are an extension of our ministry and members of God's family. They are God's gift to us . . . to care for and nurture. I cannot in my wildest dreams imagine a God who would require me to deprive a child of basic daily needs because of a preconceived, irrevocable notion in my head that our giving to our church should not be examined and reevaluated periodically.

Don't read me wrong here. Double tithing is a wonderful thing. And it may be right for you and others, too. I hope, and I make it my prayer that we will be able to do it someday, too.

We would *never* question what we consider the clear word of God for our lives: to tithe to the full amount.

Sheila and I both know, if we face a cash flow problem *now*, the tithe is no longer an issue. The house will go. Another car will go. Private Christian school will go. *But the tithe will stay!* I have seen the face of God on our lives and we *shall not* depart from it now.

It doesn't cost any money to play together as a couple. We don't have to go to movies on date night. We can go for walks. We don't have to go to fancy restaurants. We can relax just as easily over a cup of coffee at McDonald's. We don't have to go to expensive theme parks. We can take the boys to the park, we can play catch, we can borrow books from the library. Sometimes cheaper *is* better.

As we have been faithful to God, He has been faithful to us. He has shown us that Christian marriages, like the Christian life, thrive better if we make the time to play, pray, and pay.

34

All Work and No Praise!

"The water's hot! It's not going to boil any harder than it is now." My husband never fails to let me know when the tea kettle is ready.

"Okay! Okay! I'm coming!" I call from the laundry room. "Put the stove on warm for me, will ya?"

I stuff the last load of laundry of the day into the dryer and mentally check through my list of things to do. Lunches made? Check. Shirts ironed? Check. Dishwasher on? Check. Homework set out? Check. All done. I got it all done. I made it through another day, and checked everything off successfully.

Now it's time for *me!* I turn off the late news, make my cup of instant mocha, grab my favorite book or magazine, a pad of paper, and run my nightly bubble bath. This is undoubtedly my favorite time of the day. I slip into the warm, fragrant water and indulge in a moment of sheer luxury. I read to my heart's content. I sip leisurely on my soothing mocha. I stay as long as I want. My day is over. My work is done. I rest my head on the back of the tub and close my eyes, just for minute.

Somewhere in the foggy distance, I hear Jim calling, "Are you asleep? How long are you going to be in there?"

"Hmmm?" Jim's voice awakens me, but I'll never admit it. "I'll be out in a minute." Calgon takes me away, all right, straight to dreamland. I'm usually so tired by the time I get to take my bath that I sleep through the whole experience. No wonder, since I've been on the go since 6:30 in the morning. I'm lucky if I've taken time out for a sit-down lunch.

Between the wee hours of the morning and "The Tonight Show," I have worn many hats. On a typical day, I need to be a nutrition expert—making sure my meals include all four food groups, including beta carotene and fiber, and are low in saturated fat and sodium. I will have to be an educator—it takes a master's degree in education these days to help the kids with their homework. I'm a home manager—is it possible to computerize an inventory list of clean versus dirty clothes? I'm also a child-development expert—with special emphasis on toddlers to pre-adolescents. And I'm a diplomatic peacemaker—boys *love* to fight, and I've lost count of how many times I've inherited the earth.

Before I call it a day, before I slip between the cool sheets, I make out my list of things to do for tomorrow. It's folly to try to make my list in the morning. That is the busiest part of the day—rounding up four little boys, four little lunch boxes, eight little shoes. "Eat your breakfast. Did you brush your teeth? That bed is *not* made; it's thrown together! Let's go over that spelling list one more time. Where's your homework? I saw you do it. I checked it over. It must be here somewhere! Come on, it's getting late. *Let's go!*" I don't have a moment to think, much less make a careful, prioritized list of things to do.

I look over my list. There's something I've forgotten. What is it? A book overdue? No, that's not it. Field trip permission slip? No, that's not it either. I search my memory banks for the troublesome task that I am afraid I will forget to do. I come up blank. Something's missing. Something's wrong.

My list is out of balance. It's missing something important. Suddenly I remember it. In my single days I used to include quiet time, worship time, and personal Bible study in my lists. But in the last few years I've been omitting it. Why? I'm busy trying to be an excellent mother, writer, wife, and friend. But in the final analysis, is this what Christ wants from me?

What one thing does God want from me? Why did He create me? The Bible is clear. It states that we were created to worship and praise God. Jesus said it when He visited Mary and Martha. When Mary chose to worship at Jesus' feet while Martha scurried around, Jesus said, "Mary has chosen that good part."

I imagine Jesus coming to my house. I know what I would do. I would make a lemon pie. I am without doubt a Martha. No question. I am guilty as charged. My list of things to do convicts me. It opens my eyes to what God wants from me. He wants me to worship Him. He wants me to praise Him. He wants me to thank Him.

It's not easy keeping my priorities in line. There are so many distractions, not to mention emergencies. Have you ever tried to have a quiet time? Do your children interrupt too? No matter how early you get up?

Yet I know that all God wants from me is my worship. So I am taking more trips to the park where I feel God's presence. I am singing worship songs with my boys in the car on the way to school. (After all, I want them to get the message too. Life is more than getting A's on spelling tests.) I am a more patient mother; I am a more sensitive wife when I have taken the time daily to worship Jesus. I pray that God will never take away the emptiness that reminds me to turn my eyes to Him, for in the final analysis, it is His love, His patience, His wisdom that will keep my home balanced, complete, and together.

35

Lost and Found

My life changed dramatically once Jesus entered my life and alcohol left. Fortunately I lived long enough to discover this grace. Alcohol was a life-threatening problem for me. I didn't consider it a problem at the time. But it had become a way of life. I am greatly encouraged to see a growing public awareness against drunk driving and the abuse of drugs and all forms of alcohol since those days. And I am very grateful for the changes that have come into my life since then.

Long before I met Sheila, I spent all of my spare time partying. Sometimes my friends and I partied every night of the week. Of course, Friday and Saturday nights were always the high point. In fact, quite often, the entire day on a Saturday we would be sodden in beer, wine, or other alcoholic beverage. "Lost weekends" are their popular name.

Early in my freshman year at college I had my first "drunk." Three of us had each secured a bottle of wine. We had the free run of a house—parents were away, I think—or at least we felt the freedom to indulge. I remember little except totally losing all control. We drank fast and furious. We all got sick and vomited wherever. I woke up the next morning on the front yard—I had passed out.

It was early spring, not yet summer. The nights and early mornings were chilly. But that had not affected my behavior, nor apparently, my ability to pass out on the lawn and sleep throughout the night on the cold wet grass. Of course, "sleeping" on the lawn with several of my buddies, whom I saw as I looked around, seemed quite comical and "macho" at the time. And it became our tendency to brag about such exploits as my drinking years went on.

Of course, sleeping on a cold lawn did not satisfy the macho drive for long. Soon we were driving, stealing, and involved in quite a number of activities that I pray God will protect my children from. Was it God's grace or luck that saved me from the countless times we drove fast and recklessly, while intoxicated? As painful as it is to recall how lost I was in those days, I pray that I will never forget what God spared me from:

• I remember screeching tires as I pushed the '57 Chevy hard into every turn of the mountain road. I stayed on the road that night.

• I remember the day a friend bought a brand new Porsche. He asked me if I wanted to try it out. Of course we were both drunk by that time. I slid sideways off the road at a high speed. Somehow I managed to avoid wrapping the exquisite automobile around a pole. Once again I'd been spared.

• I remember driving to San Francisco, alone, stopping to get some gasoline and using the restroom at the filling station. The next thing I remember was being awakened from a blacked-out condition. I was lying in front of my car, gas nozzle still in the tank. I came to, rushed to the driver's seat and tore off before anyone could try to stop me or call the police.

• I remember driving down the wrong side of the road at one o'clock in the morning after a sixty-mile trip home from Los Angeles. I got a ticket in my driveway. But the officer never checked my condition. He only told me to go to bed immediately.

• I remember rocketing down a dirt road in the desert in the middle of the night behind a friend on the back of his motorcycle. We hit something that threw the cycle down. We both tumbled and laughed. Great fun! We didn't notice the large rocks all around us. It never occurred to us what we had nearly done to ourselves. We rocketed back to the house where we threw down one more brew.

• I remember waking up in the morning with *absolutely* no idea as to where I had driven in the last four hours of our trip. We were stopped by a policeman early in our journey. He had warned me to stay on my side of the road. He had not inspected the car or its occupants. Consequently, he hadn't noticed our obvious intoxication. Why he let me go on is something I've never fully understood. But I do know one thing. When I woke up the next morning, I could hardly sit up. I still carried some of the intoxicants from the previous night. My head spun. It hurt. My insides ached. My mind raced as best it could, given its condition. *What had happened? Where had we gone? Did we all get home safely?*

I can't tell you how grateful I am that Jesus snatched me from destruction. He brought love and meaning and forgiveness into my life when I needed it most. And He saved me from the jaws of alcohol. He wiped out substance abuse from my life. It didn't happen overnight. I began to drink less and less. As I became involved in Bible study groups and learned more and more about the man I had met on the bus, I no longer needed alcohol as I had before. By the time I started dating Sheila, I only enjoyed an occasional beer.

But this, too, would soon change. Jesus, at my invitation, had taken up residence in my soul. As He ministered to the inner me—my need to hide behind the bliss of liquor was being replaced by a more emotionally stable personality.

I have seen alcohol and/or drugs hauled into the marriage relationship. Substance abuse, in my opinion, only complicates any problem—it is the solution to none.

One or two of my friends continued to use alcohol, and it troubled me to see the terribly negative impact it had on each of their marriages. With great courage and immense effort, I watched them walk away from alcoholism and restore their relationships with loving, forgiving wives. I'm grateful that my abstinence served as a positive example and that I could be there for them when their marriages came close to crashing in.

Acknowledgment is the first step to recovery. Admission is the first step toward growth. Confession is the first step toward forgiveness. Before you give up on marriage, ask God if there is some area that needs to be relinquished. Ask God to give you the courage to acknowledge a change that needs to be made. You can do it. You can grow through this. Don't run away from the pain. Reach out and get help—you can make it. All things are possible with God!

36

To the Prettiest Girl in the Restaurant

I can't tell you how many times I've heard my father say, "If you fail to plan, you're planning to fail." I've applied those words of wisdom to my career, my vocation, even my diet. But, until recently, I never applied them to my relationship with Jim.

This is remarkable, considering the elaborate plans we made when we were first dating. Jim was just as creative as I was when it came to courtship. One night he really outdid himself.

"Where are we going?" I asked as the little car sped along the highway. Jim and I had been dating several months now.

"It's a surprise," he murmured. I knew that it was useless trying to drag a secret from Jim's lips. They were sealed tighter than any bank vault.

I was ready for a surprise. It was obvious that Jim was heading in the opposite direction of our usual haunts. I couldn't imagine where he was taking me, but it was fun trying. I thought of some of our favorite places—the places where we usually enjoyed being alone—dining graciously and casually!

The sky was growing dark. Black clouds hung heavy, like a thick blanket. Jim's little car hugged the curving road that wound through the beautiful California canyons. Golden shafts of fading light managed to break through the threatening sky here and there, illuminating great golden, green wedges of landscape. The glorious contrasts of brilliant, setting beams of light, breaking through dark, ominous shadows, made for a spectacular drive. We couldn't have seen more beautiful scenery in any movie theater, and this was ours for the looking. A free gift. We took in the beauty and relished the majesty of God's world in silence.

After forty-five minutes or so of breathtaking beauty, Jim pulled off and turned into the parking lot of an obscure diner. Motor homes, trucks, and motorcycles dotted the parking lot. This greasy spoon wasn't my idea of a special night out. I was beginning to feel disappointed and just a little confused.

"Wait here," he ordered with a twinkle in his eyes.

What's he up to now? I thought. I strained to see Jim through the windows. I could barely make out his profile, standing by the counter. He was talking to the hostess. *Is she setting up a special table for us?* I wondered. It was not the kind of restaurant where one would make special requests. There wasn't much they could do with linoleum, tin napkin holders, and dented salt and pepper shakers. *Maybe he's asking for directions,* I thought hopefully.

It seemed like I waited forever. Finally he emerged from that old diner. He was carrying styrofoam platters. "What in the world!?" I muttered. I put on the bravest face I could muster and smiled at him as he opened the door. "What's this?"

"This is dinner," he said. He handed me the large white, squeaky containers and said, "I have to go back for the rest. Hold these."

As he returned to the scene of the crime, I fought back a bitter disappointment. This was not what I had in mind. "Oh, don't be so selfish!" I admonished myself. "You know that Jim can't always afford those fancy places."

I continued to talk myself out of the blues as the delicious odor of fried chicken wafted through the little car. The warmth of the hot meal seeped through the containers. My mouth began to water. Jim was running across the parking lot with two more large containers, smiling broadly. "Well," he said as he settled himself and the steaming packages. "It sure smells good."

"Mmmm," I agreed as heartily as I could.

"No fair peeking," he admonished as he put the car in gear and zoomed off down the road once again.

I was growing more confused by the moment. Where were we going? What were we going to do with this food? As we wound up the hills, a heavy rain began to fall. Great drops fell on us as we bravely climbed the slick, wet road. The headlights searched the dark curves as we groped ever higher and higher. Finally, Jim said, "Here we are!"

Here we are?! I thought to myself incredulously. Here we are—in no-wheres-ville. There was nothing in sight, except for the glorious view that suddenly came in sight. Jim turned onto a turn-out and settled the car so that it looked down over the twinkling city. Through the raindrops we could still make out the glistening city lights.

He reached into the glove compartment and pulled out a candle and some matches. He lit the candle, handed me a card, and gave me a kiss. The card said, "To the prettiest girl in the restaurant."

I laughed, entranced. I certainly was the prettiest girl there; heaven knows I was the *only* girl there! The candle flickered and glowed in the shelter of our little private place. Misty swirls rising from the chicken, biscuits, and

181

gravy gradually draped the windows like curtains. The outside world grew more and more distant. After a while it was as if we were the only two people in the world— on top of the world—together, alone.

That evening was one of the most romantic moments in my life. It was a gift of love from Jim. It didn't cost him very much money. But it took a little bit of planning, some creativity, and a great deal of love to put it together. It was the thought, the caring, the love that made the evening so special, that made me feel so loved.

As I remember that evening, I ponder how little planning we sometimes put into our love. We think that it will just grow without any effort. We seem to take it for granted that our love will last a lifetime. And so we stop working at it, we stop thinking up ways to make it exciting. We let our love go on its own way while we go our own way, and then we wake up one day and wonder why it's nearly gone.

When was the last time I planned a special evening for the one I love? When was the last time I made him feel loved? Not by the amount of money spent, but by the amount of time and thought? I ask myself these questions from time to time, because like everybody, life's pressures distract me from my love for Jim. I fall victim to the notion that my work, my children, my myriad duties are more important than he is. I neglect him and fail to think up ways to show him that I love him.

I don't do it on purpose. I get sidetracked by my children's needs, by work demands, deadlines, daily chores. By the time I give my best creative energies to those endeavors, it's as if there's nothing left over for Jim.

My spouse isn't happy with leftovers every night of the week. He needs, he expects, and he deserves five-star treatment from time to time. I need to put on my thinking cap, aim some of my creativity Jim's way, and come up with some fun plans. If we make a commitment to keep our love important, if we take the time to plan romantic surprises, then our love will grow and deepen— and we will be together *forever!*